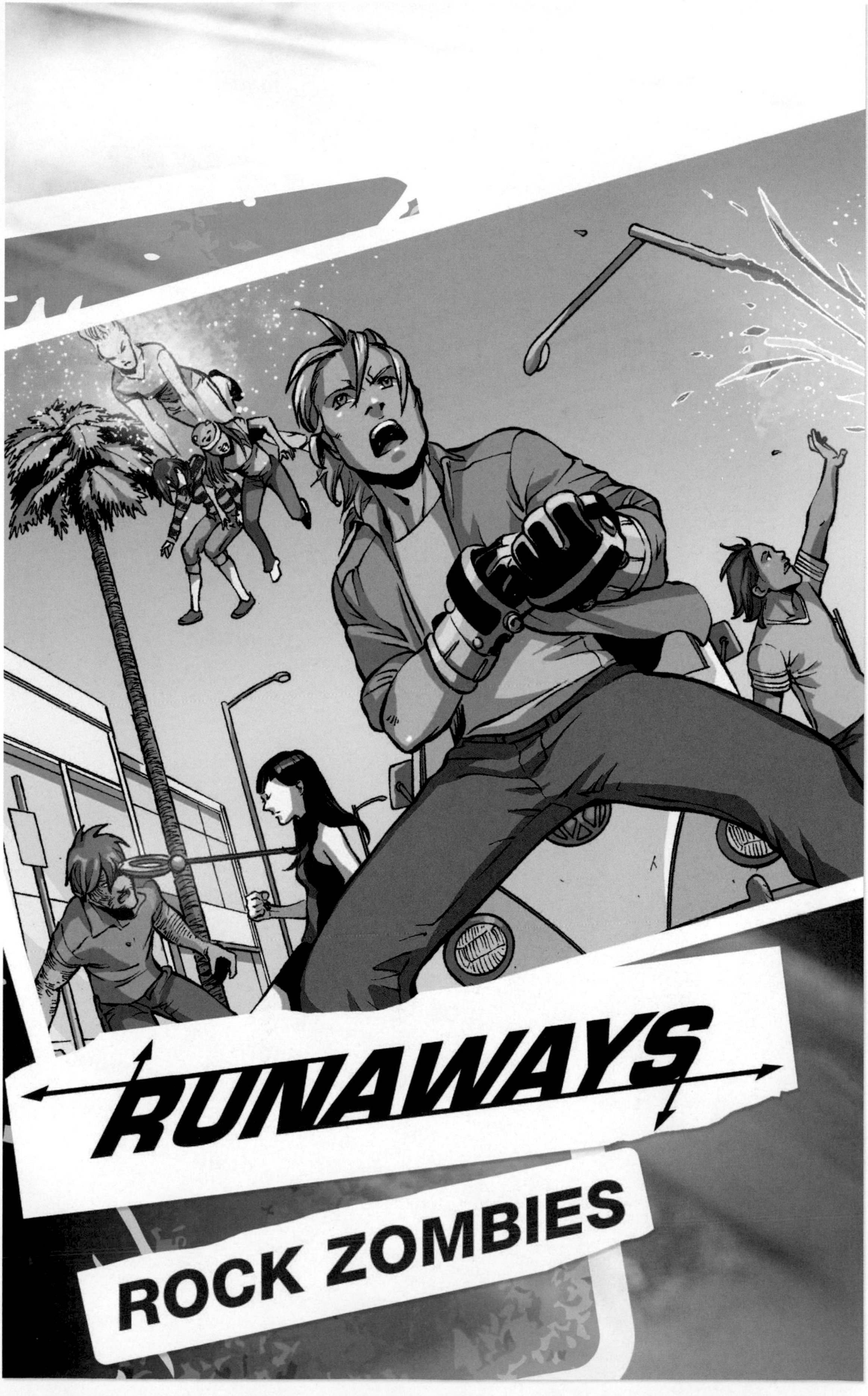
RUNAWAYS
ROCK ZOMBIES

RUNAWAYS
ROCK ZOMBIES

WRITER: **TERRY MOORE**

PENCILER: **TAKESHI MIYAZAWA**

INKERS: **TAKESHI MIYAZAWA, NORMAN LEE & CRAIG YEUNG**

COVER ART: **HUMBERTO RAMOS & CHRISTINA STRAIN**

"MOLLIFEST DESTINY"

WRITER: **CHRIS YOST**

ARTIST: **SARA PICHELLI**

"TRUTH OR DARE"

WRITER: **JAMES ASMUS**

ARTIST: **EMMA RIOS**

COVER ART: **DAVID LAFUENTE & CHRISTINA STRAIN**

COLORIST: **CHRISTINA STRAIN**

LETTERER: **VC'S JOE CARAMAGNA**

EDITORS: **NICK LOWE & DANIEL KETCHUM**

RUNAWAYS CREATED BY **BRIAN K. VAUGHAN & ADRIAN ALPHONA**

COLLECTION EDITOR: **JENNIFER GRÜNWALD**

EDITORIAL ASSISTANT: **ALEX STARBUCK**

ASSISTANT EDITORS: **CORY LEVINE & JOHN DENNING**

EDITOR, SPECIAL PROJECTS: **MARK D. BEAZLEY**

SENIOR EDITOR, SPECIAL PROJECTS: **JEFF YOUNGQUIST**

SENIOR VICE PRESIDENT OF SALES: **DAVID GABRIEL**

EDITOR IN CHIEF: **JOE QUESADA**

PUBLISHER: **DAN BUCKLEY**

EXECUTIVE PRODUCER: **ALAN FINE**

RUNAWAYS: ROCK ZOMBIES. Contains material originally published in magazine form as RUNAWAYS #7-10. First printing 2009. Hardcover ISBN# 978-0-7851-3156-4. Softcover ISBN# 978-0-7851-4074-0. Published by MARVEL PUBLISHING, INC., a subsidiary of MARVEL ENTERTAINMENT, INC. OFFICE OF PUBLICATION: 417 5th Avenue, New York, NY 10016. Copyright © 2009 Marvel Characters, Inc. All rights reserved. Hardcover: $19.99 per copy in the U.S. (GST #R127032852). Softcover: $14.99 per copy in the U.S. (GST #R127032852). Canadian Agreement #40668537. All characters featured in this issue and the distinctive names and likenesses thereof, and all related indicia are trademarks of Marvel Characters, Inc. No similarity between any of the names, characters, persons, and/or institutions in this magazine with those of any living or dead person or institution is intended, and any such similarity which may exist is purely coincidental. **Printed in the U.S.A.** ALAN FINE, CEO Marvel Publishing Division and EVP & CMO Marvel Characters B.V.; DAN BUCKLEY, President of Publishing - Print & Digital Media; JIM SOKOLOWSKI, Chief Operating Officer; DAVID GABRIEL, SVP of Publishing Sales & Circulation; DAVID BOGART, SVP of Business Affairs & Talent Management; MICHAEL PASCIULLO, VP Merchandising & Communications; JIM O'KEEFE, VP of Operations & Logistics; DAN CARR, Executive Director of Publishing Technology; JUSTIN F. GABRIE, Director of Publishing & Editorial Operations; SUSAN CRESPI, Editorial Operations Manager; ALEX MORALES, Publishing Operations Manager; STAN LEE, Chairman Emeritus. For information regarding advertising in Marvel Comics or on Marvel.com, please contact Mitch Dane, Advertising Director, at mdane@marvel.com. For Marvel subscription inquiries, please call 800-217-9158.

10 9 8 7 6 5 4 3 2 1

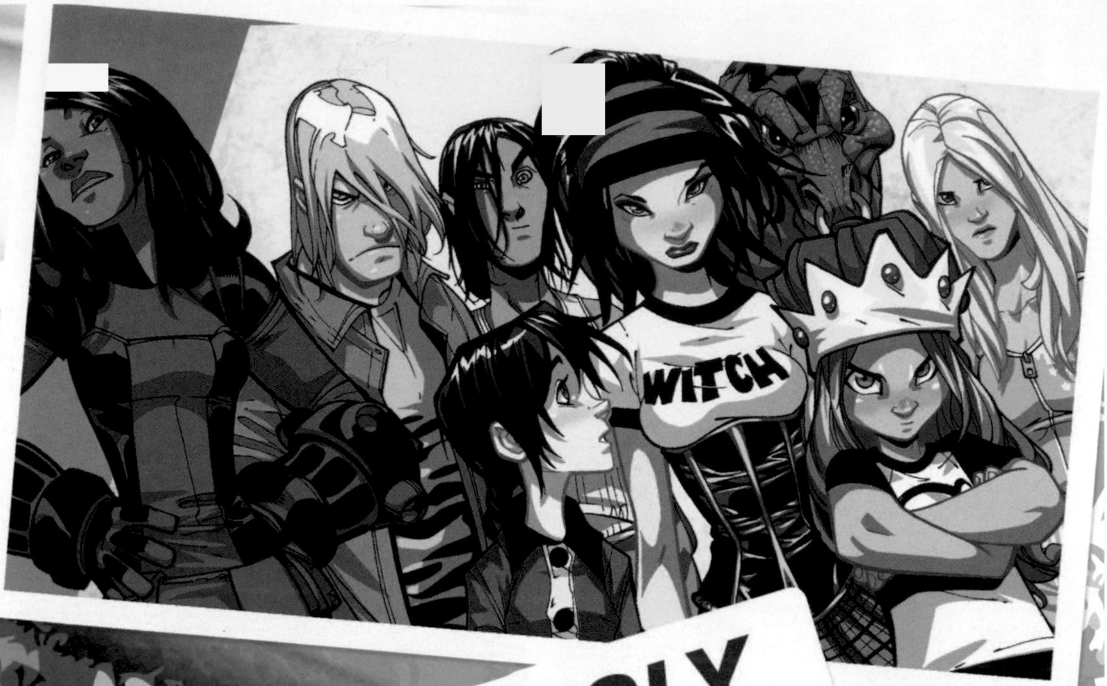
WITCH

PREVIOUSLY

AT SOME POINT IN THEIR LIVES, ALL KIDS THINK THAT THEIR PARENTS ARE EVIL. FOR MOLLY HAYES AND HER FRIENDS, THIS IS ESPECIALLY TRUE. ONE NIGHT, MOLLY AND HER FRIENDS DISCOVERED THAT THEIR PARENTS WERE A GROUP OF SUPER-POWERED CRIME BOSSES WHO CALLED THEMSELVES "THE PRIDE." USING TECHNOLOGY AND RESOURCES STOLEN FROM THEIR PARENTS, THE TEENAGERS WERE ABLE TO STOP THE PRIDE AND BREAK THEIR CRIMINAL HOLD ON LOS ANGELES. BUT THEY'VE BEEN ON THE RUN EVER SINCE.

ATTACKED BY A CREW OF MAJESDANIAN SOLDIERS INTENT ON CAPTURING THE RUNAWAYS' KAROLINA DEAN—WHOM THEY HOLD RESPONSIBLE FOR THE DESTRUCTION OF THEIR HOME PLANET—THE RUNAWAYS FIGHT BACK AND DO EVERYTHING THEY CAN TO ESCAPE. BUT WHEN THEY REALIZE THAT THIS IS A FIGHT THEY WON'T BE ABLE TO WIN, THE SHAPESHIFTING XAVIN TAKES KAROLINA'S PLACE AND WILLINGLY AGREES TO GO WITH THE MAJESDANIANS, LEAVING HER FELLOW RUNAWAYS BEHIND.

7

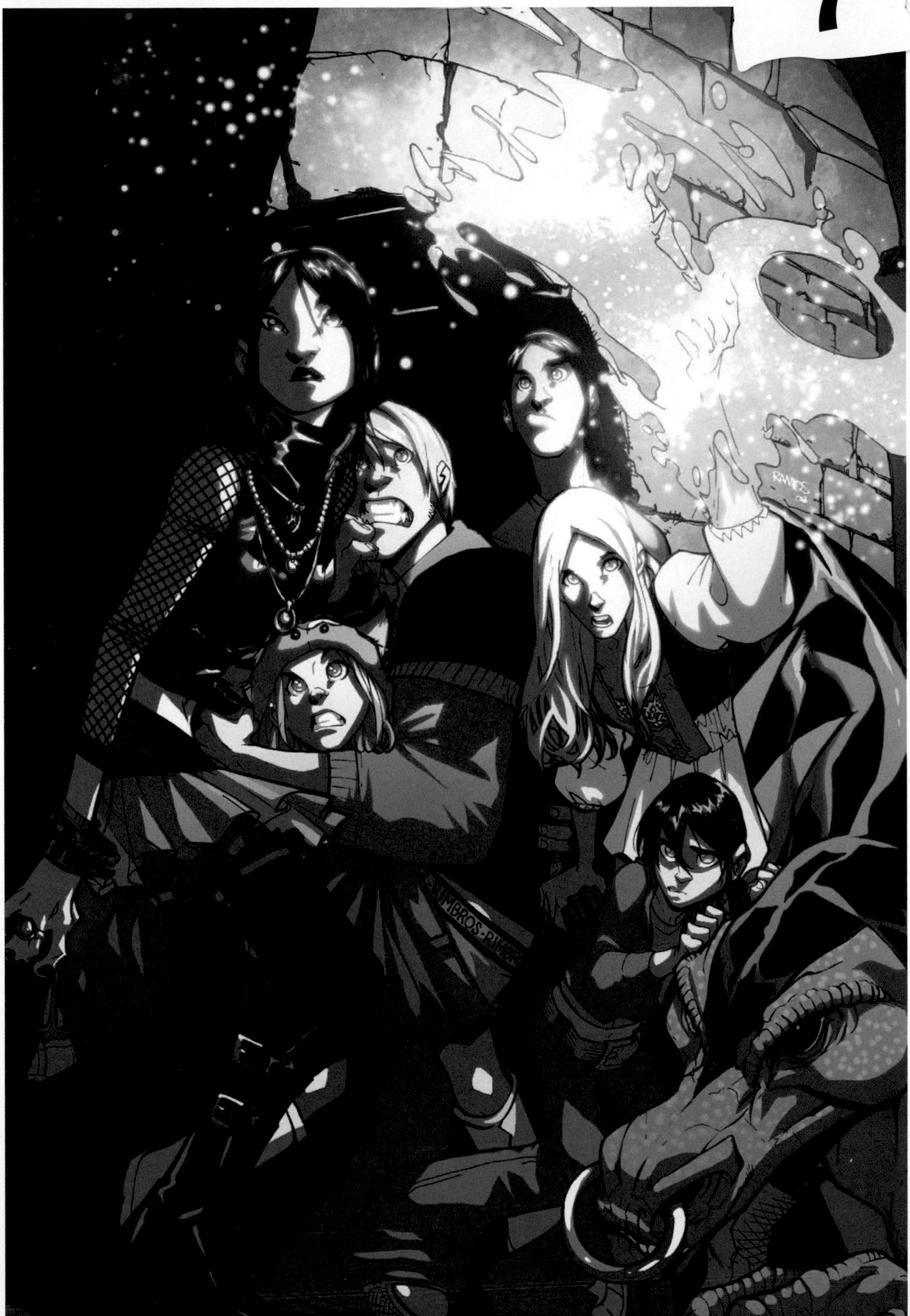

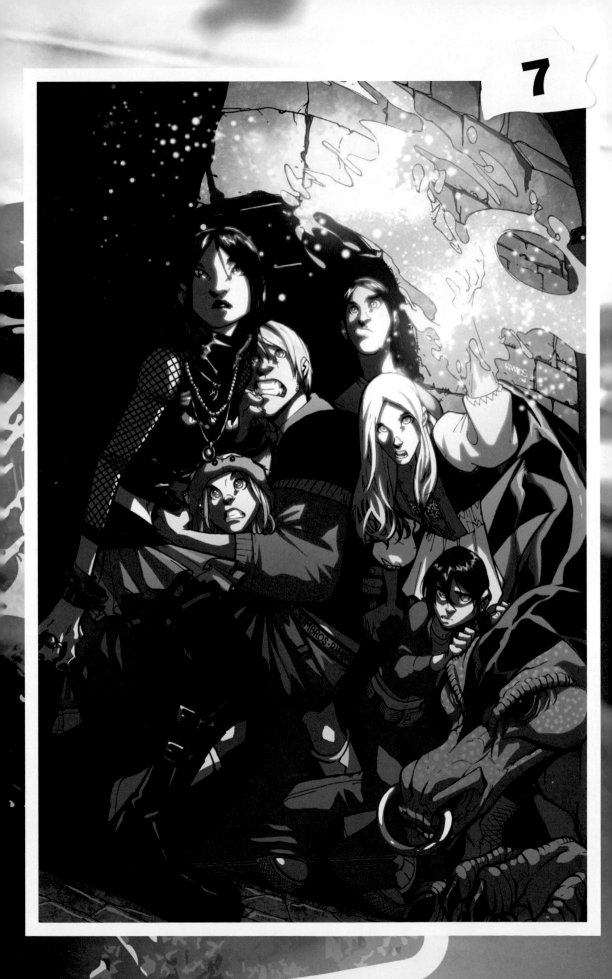

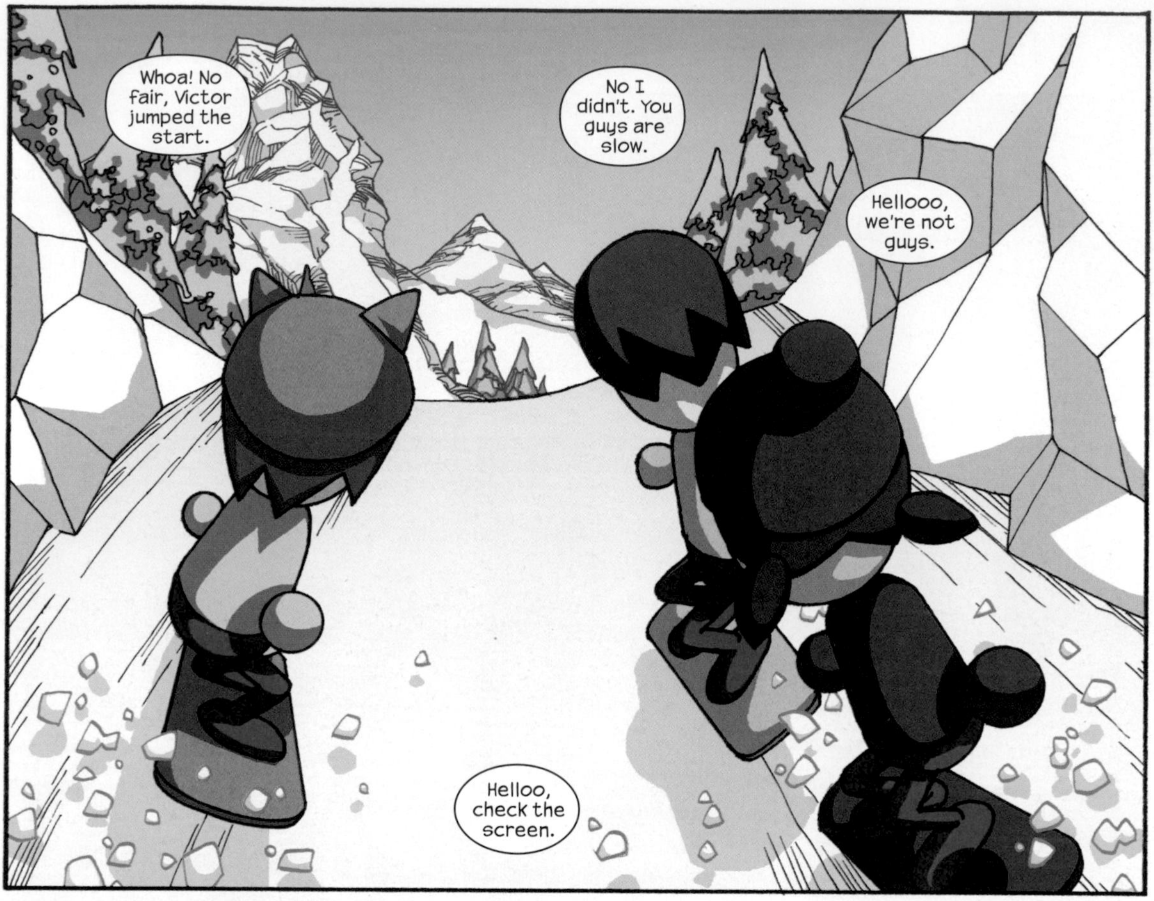
Whoa! No fair, Victor jumped the start.
No I didn't. You guys are slow.
Hellooo, we're not guys.
Helloo, check the screen.

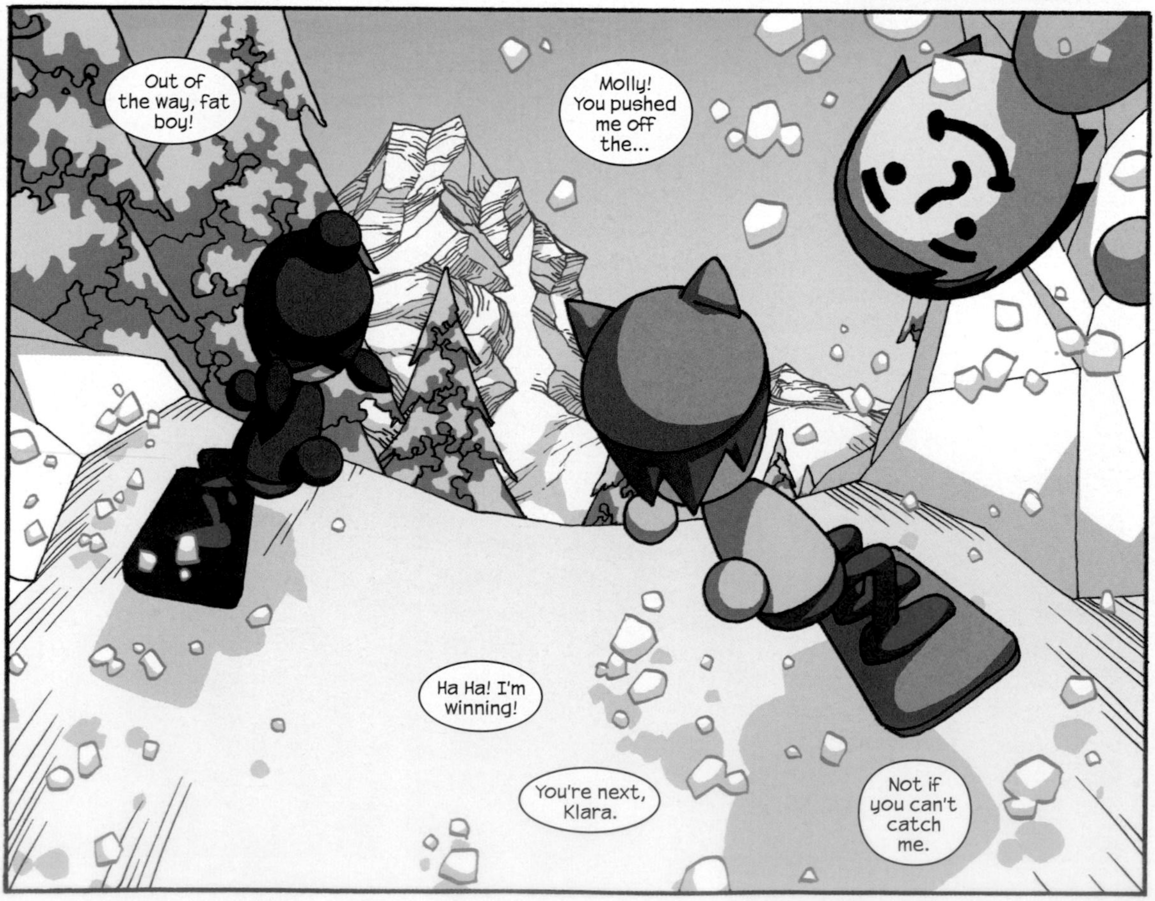
Out of the way, fat boy!
Molly! You pushed me off the...
Ha Ha! I'm winning!
You're next, Klara.
Not if you can't catch me.

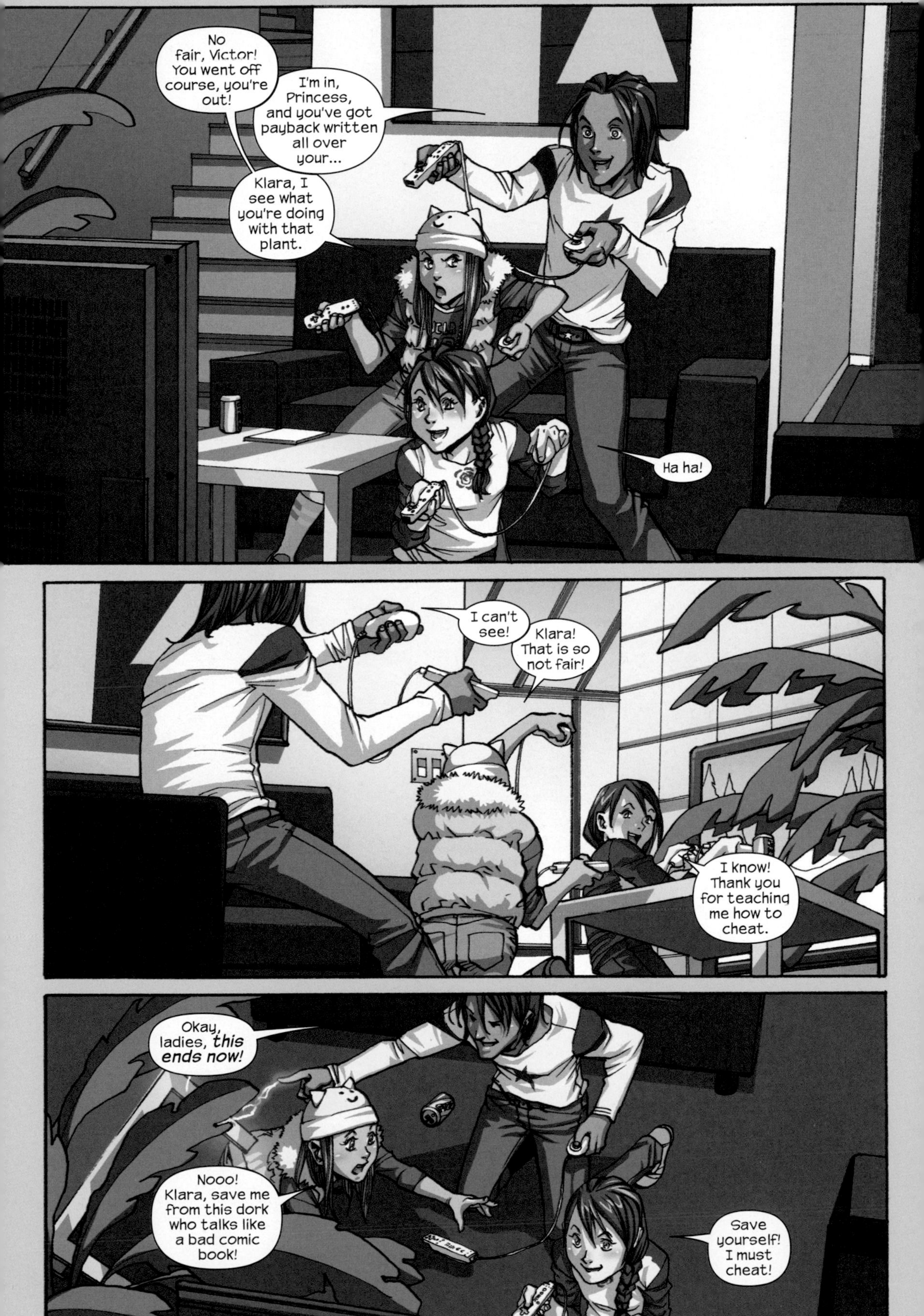
No fair, Victor! You went off course, you're out!
I'm in, Princess, and you've got payback written all over your...
Klara, I see what you're doing with that plant.
Ha ha!
I can't see!
Klara! That is so not fair!
I know! Thank you for teaching me how to cheat.
Okay, ladies, *this ends now!*
Nooo! Klara, save me from this dork who talks like a bad comic book!
Save yourself! I must cheat!

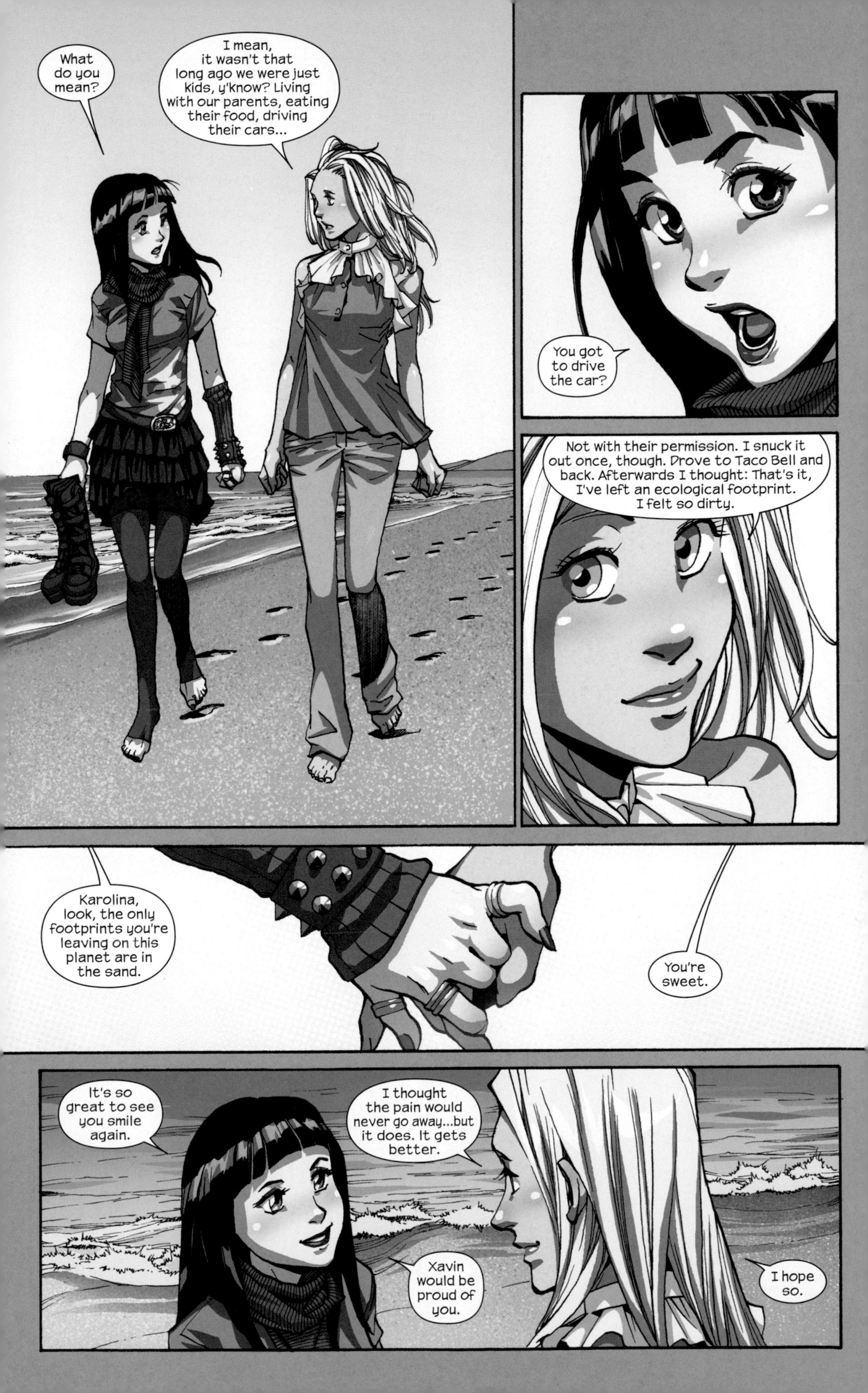
What do you mean?
I mean, it wasn't that long ago we were just kids, y'know? Living with our parents, eating their food, driving their cars...
You got to drive the car?
Not with their permission. I snuck it out once, though. Drove to Taco Bell and back. Afterwards I thought: That's it, I've left an ecological footprint. I felt so dirty.
Karolina, look, the only footprints you're leaving on this planet are in the sand.
You're sweet.
It's so great to see you smile again.
I thought the pain would never go away...but it does. It gets better.
Xavin would be proud of you.
I hope so.

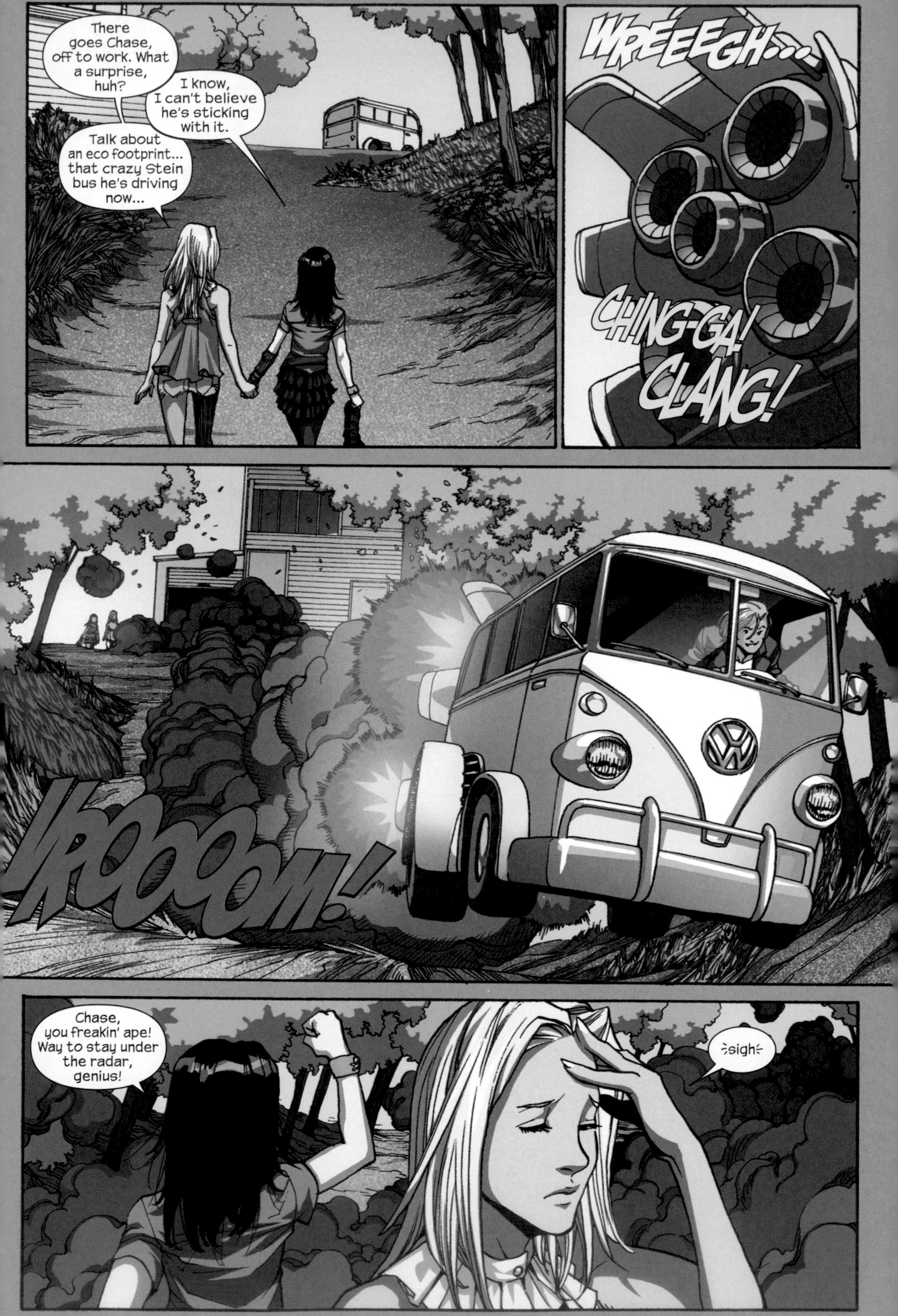
There goes Chase, off to work. What a surprise, huh?
I know, I can't believe he's sticking with it.
Talk about an eco footprint... that crazy Stein bus he's driving now...
WREEEGH...
CHING-GA! CLANG!
VROOOOM!
Chase, you freakin' ape! Way to stay under the radar, genius!
sigh

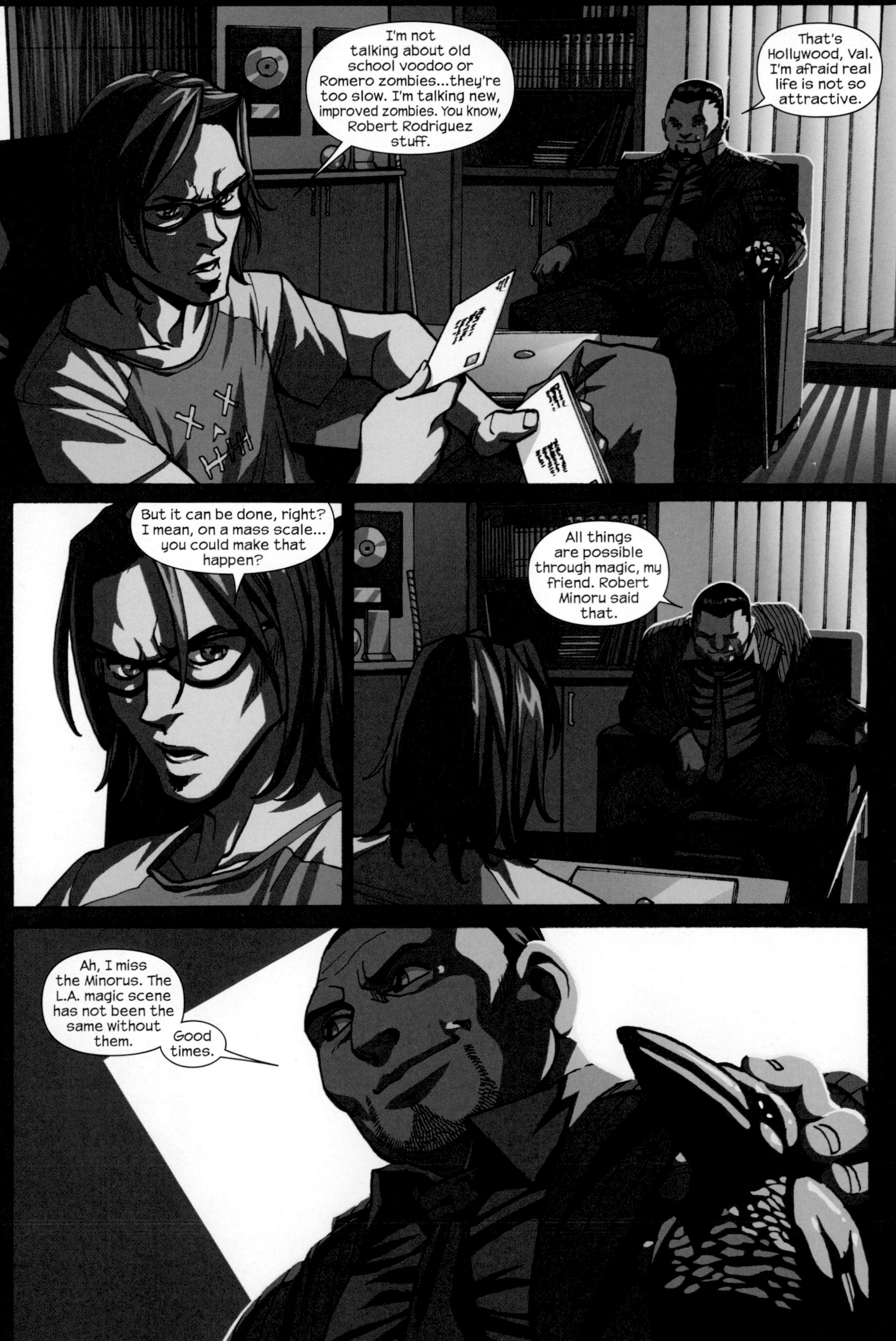
I'm not talking about old school voodoo or Romero zombies...they're too slow. I'm talking new, improved zombies. You know, Robert Rodriguez stuff.
That's Hollywood, Val. I'm afraid real life is not so attractive.
But it can be done, right? I mean, on a mass scale... you could make that happen?
All things are possible through magic, my friend. Robert Minoru said that.
Ah, I miss the Minorus. The L.A. magic scene has not been the same without them.
Good times.

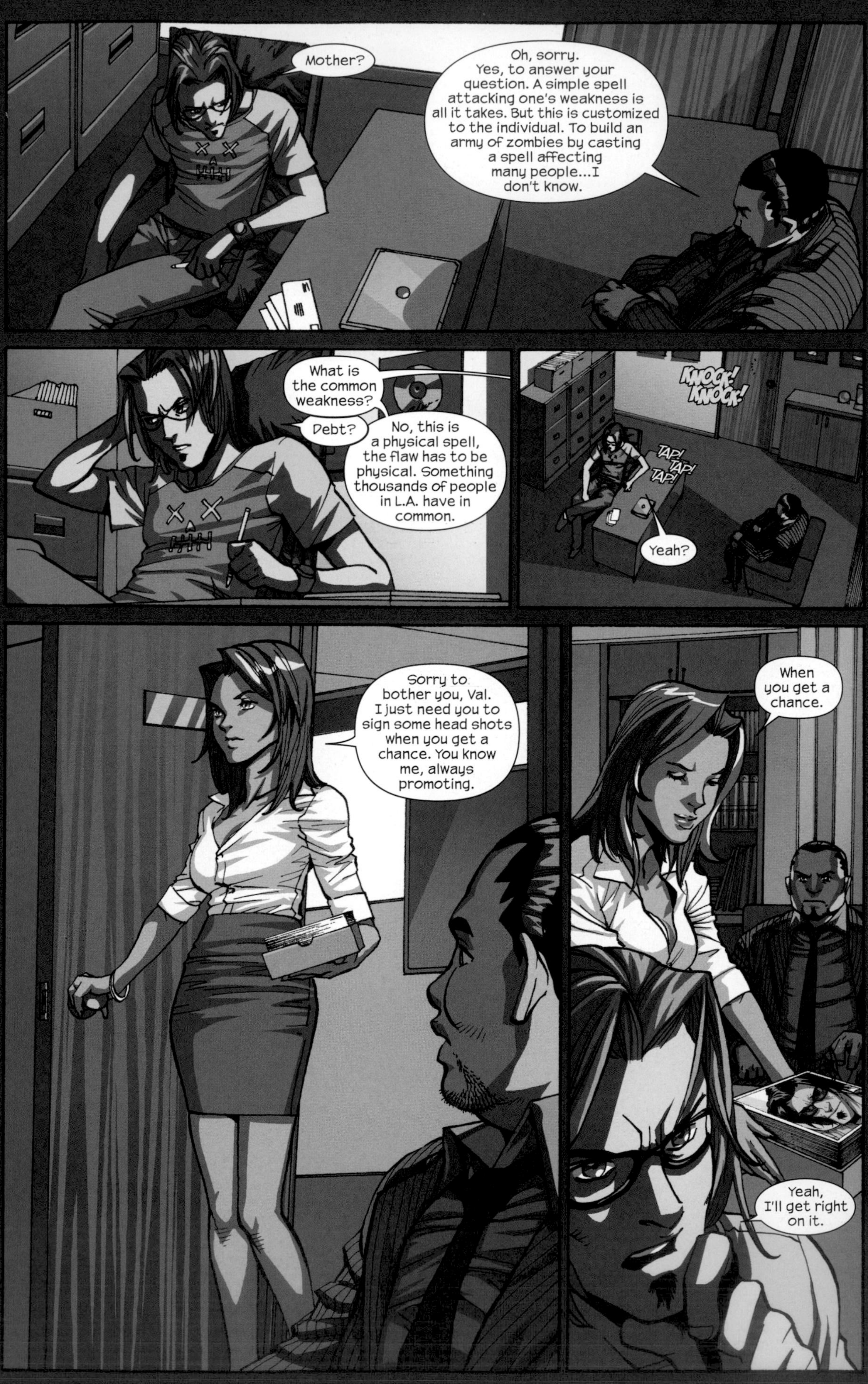
Mother?
Oh, sorry. Yes, to answer your question. A simple spell attacking one's weakness is all it takes. But this is customized to the individual. To build an army of zombies by casting a spell affecting many people...I don't know.
What is the common weakness?
Debt?
No, this is a physical spell, the flaw has to be physical. Something thousands of people in L.A. have in common.
KNOCK! KNOCK!
TAP! TAP! TAP!
Yeah?
Sorry to bother you, Val. I just need you to sign some head shots when you get a chance. You know me, always promoting.
When you get a chance.
Yeah, I'll get right on it.

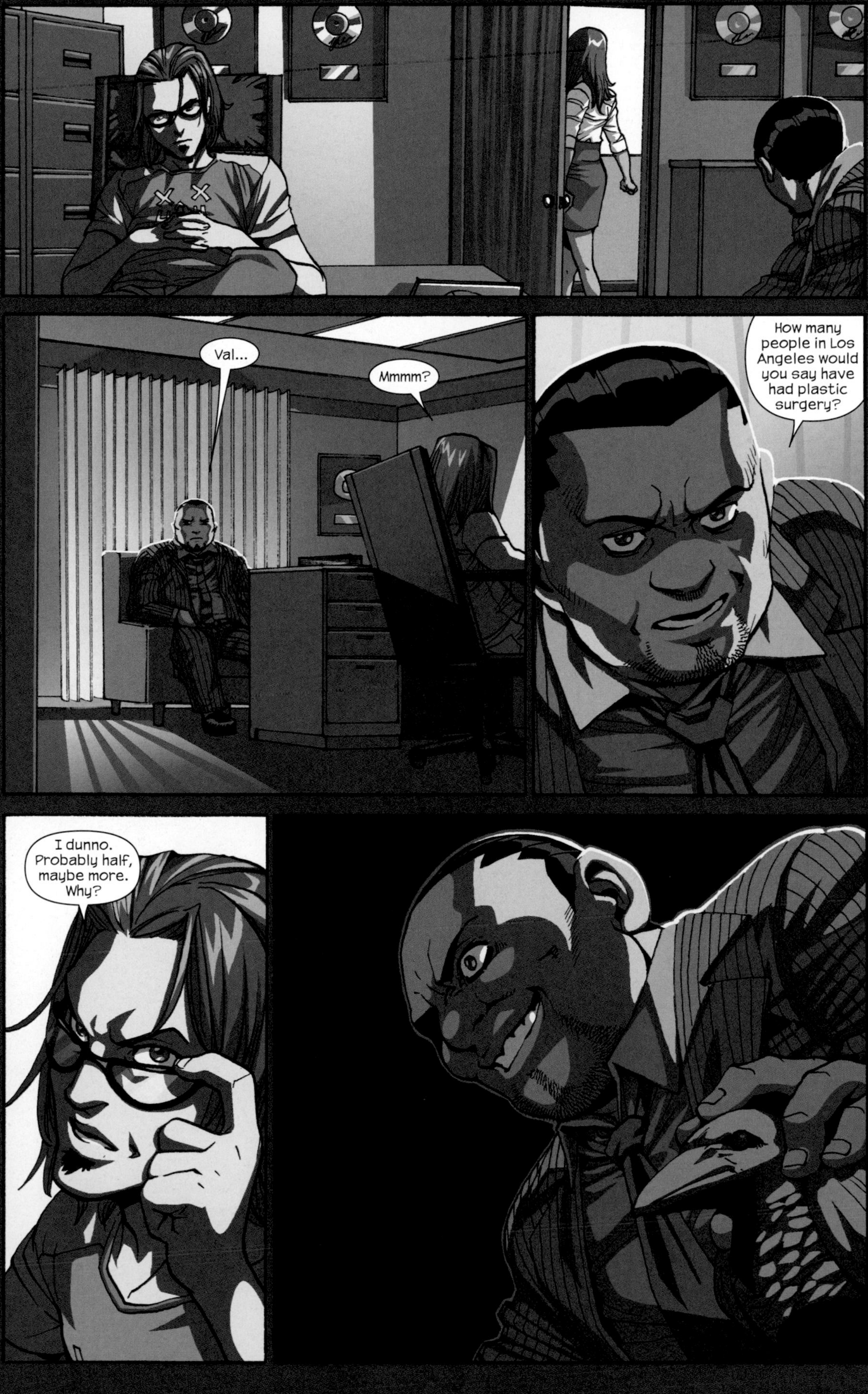
Val...
Mmmm?
How many people in Los Angeles would you say have had plastic surgery?
I dunno. Probably half, maybe more. Why?

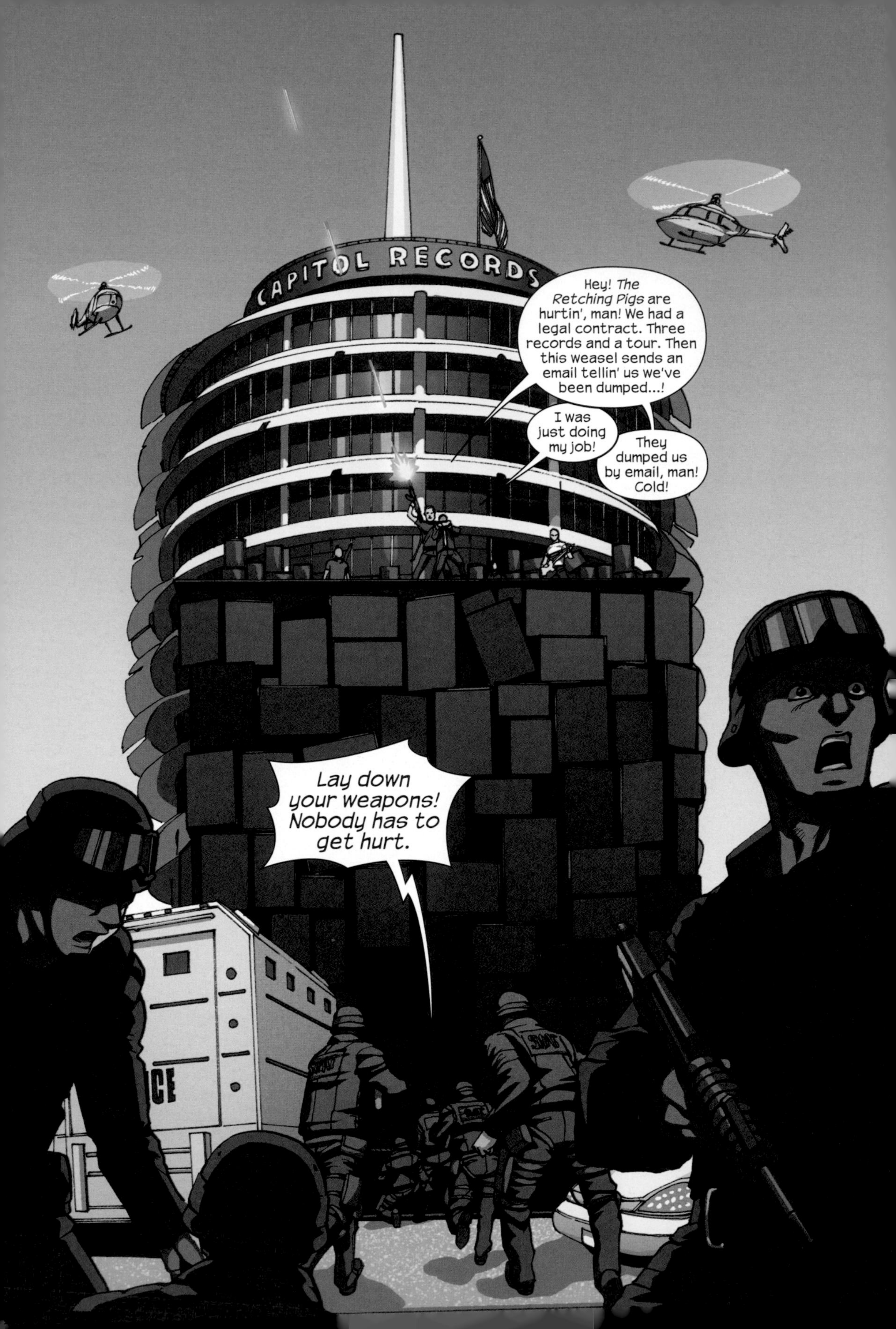
CAPITOL RECORDS
Hey! *The Retching Pigs* are hurtin', man! We had a legal contract. Three records and a tour. Then this weasel sends an email tellin' us we've been dumped...!
I was just doing my job!
They dumped us by email, man! Cold!
Lay down your weapons! Nobody has to get hurt.

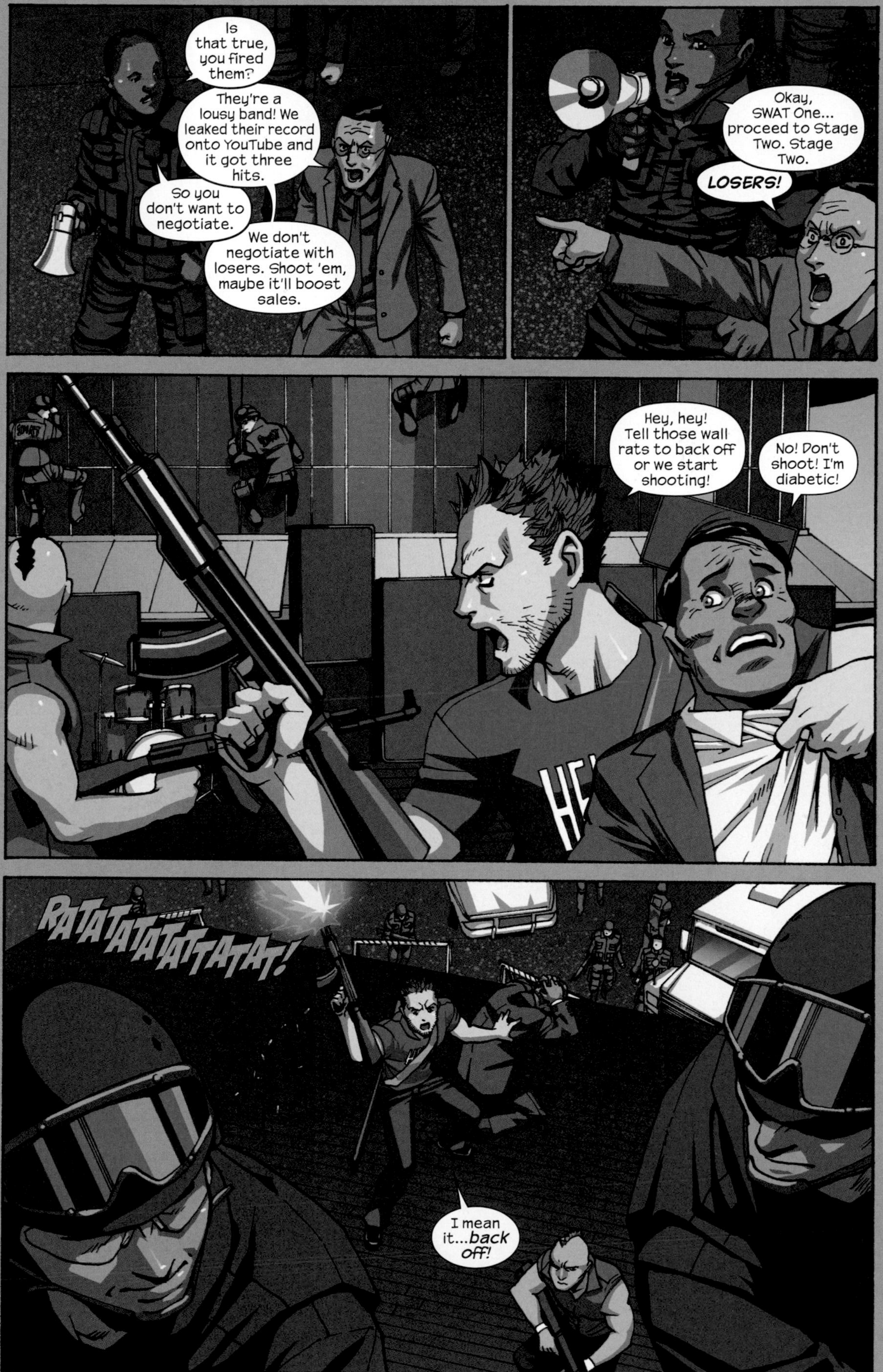
Is that true, you fired them?
They're a lousy band! We leaked their record onto YouTube and it got three hits.
So you don't want to negotiate.
We don't negotiate with losers. Shoot 'em, maybe it'll boost sales.
Okay, SWAT One... proceed to Stage Two. Stage Two.
LOSERS!
Hey, hey! Tell those wall rats to back off or we start shooting!
No! Don't shoot! I'm diabetic!
RATATATATATTTATAT!
I mean it...back off!

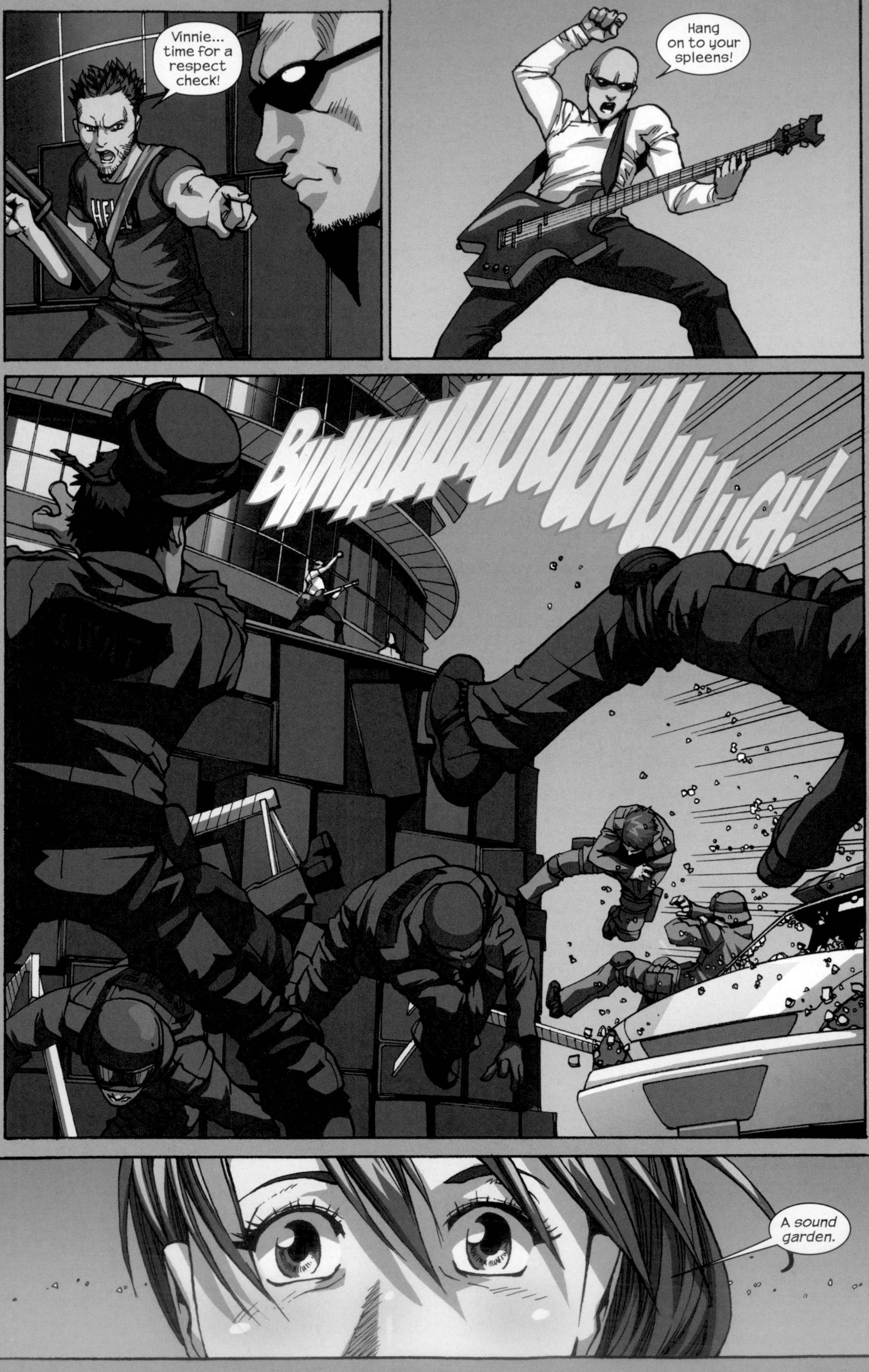
Vinnie... time for a respect check!
Hang on to your spleens!
BWUAAAAUUUUUUUUUGH!
A sound garden.

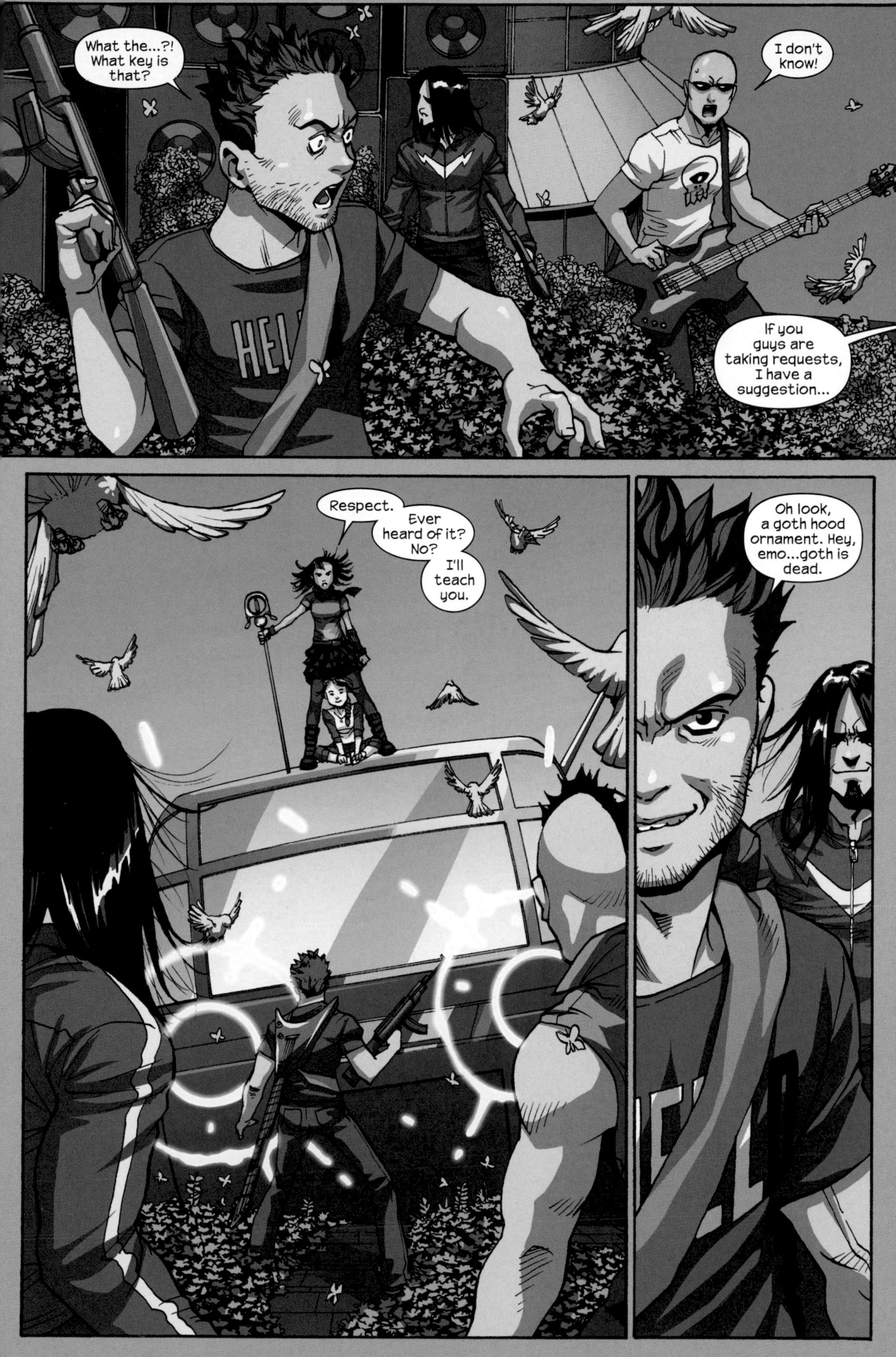

What the...?! What key is that?
I don't know!
If you guys are taking requests, I have a suggestion...
Respect.
Ever heard of it? No?
I'll teach you.
Oh look, a goth hood ornament. Hey, emo...goth is dead.

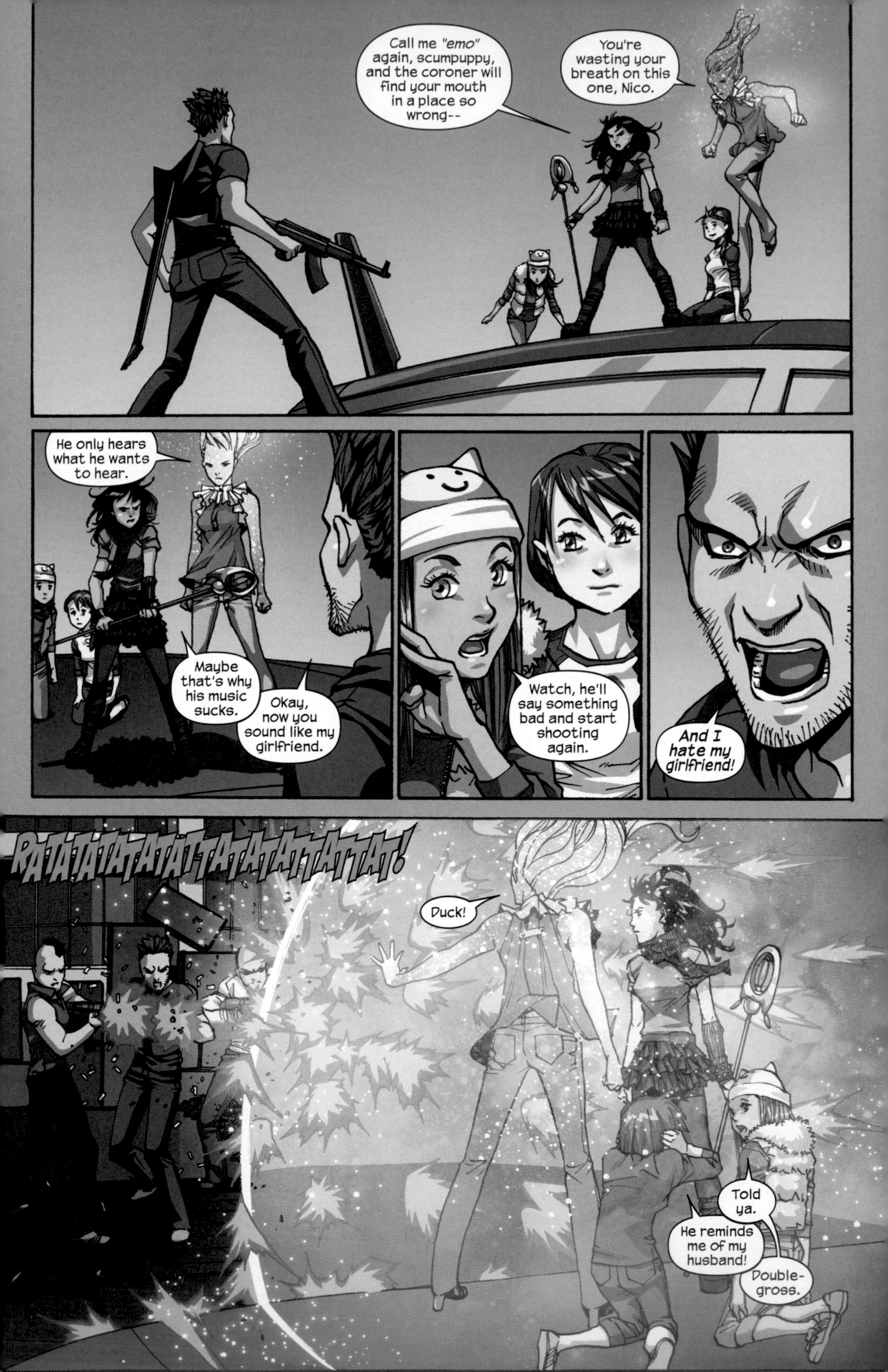
Call me "emo" again, scumpuppy, and the coroner will find your mouth in a place so wrong--
You're wasting your breath on this one, Nico.
He only hears what he wants to hear.
Maybe that's why his music sucks.
Okay, now you sound like my girlfriend.
Watch, he'll say something bad and start shooting again.
And I hate my girlfriend!
RATATATATATATTATATATTATTAT!
Duck!
Told ya.
He reminds me of my husband!
Double-gross.

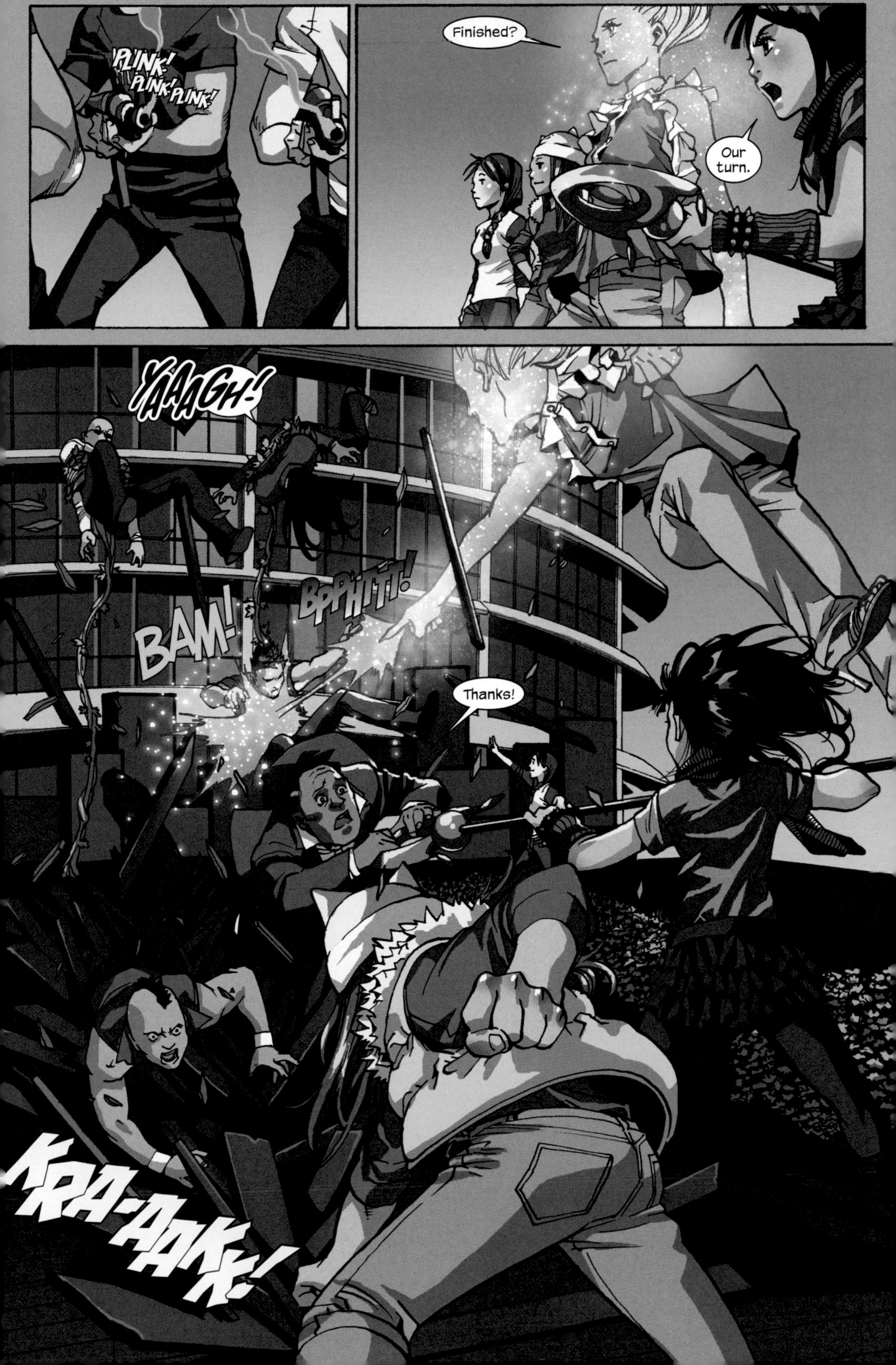
PLINK! PLINK! PLINK!
Finished?
Our turn.
YAAAGH!
BAM!
BPPHTTT!
Thanks!
KRA-AAKK!

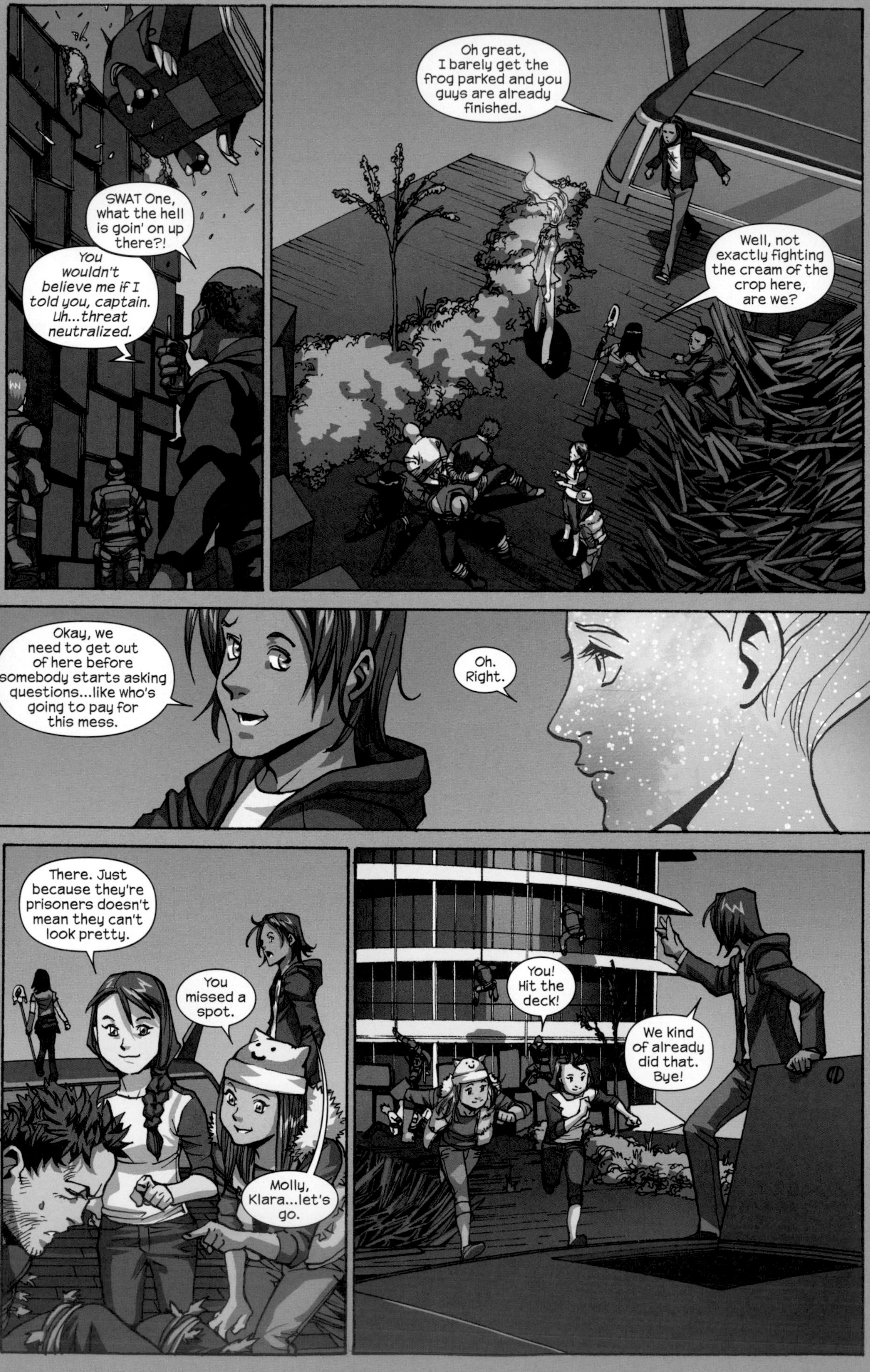
SWAT One, what the hell is goin' on up there?!
You wouldn't believe me if I told you, captain. Uh...threat neutralized.
Oh great, I barely get the frog parked and you guys are already finished.
Well, not exactly fighting the cream of the crop here, are we?
Okay, we need to get out of here before somebody starts asking questions...like who's going to pay for this mess.
Oh. Right.
There. Just because they're prisoners doesn't mean they can't look pretty.
You missed a spot.
Molly, Klara...let's go.
You! Hit the deck!
We kind of already did that. Bye!

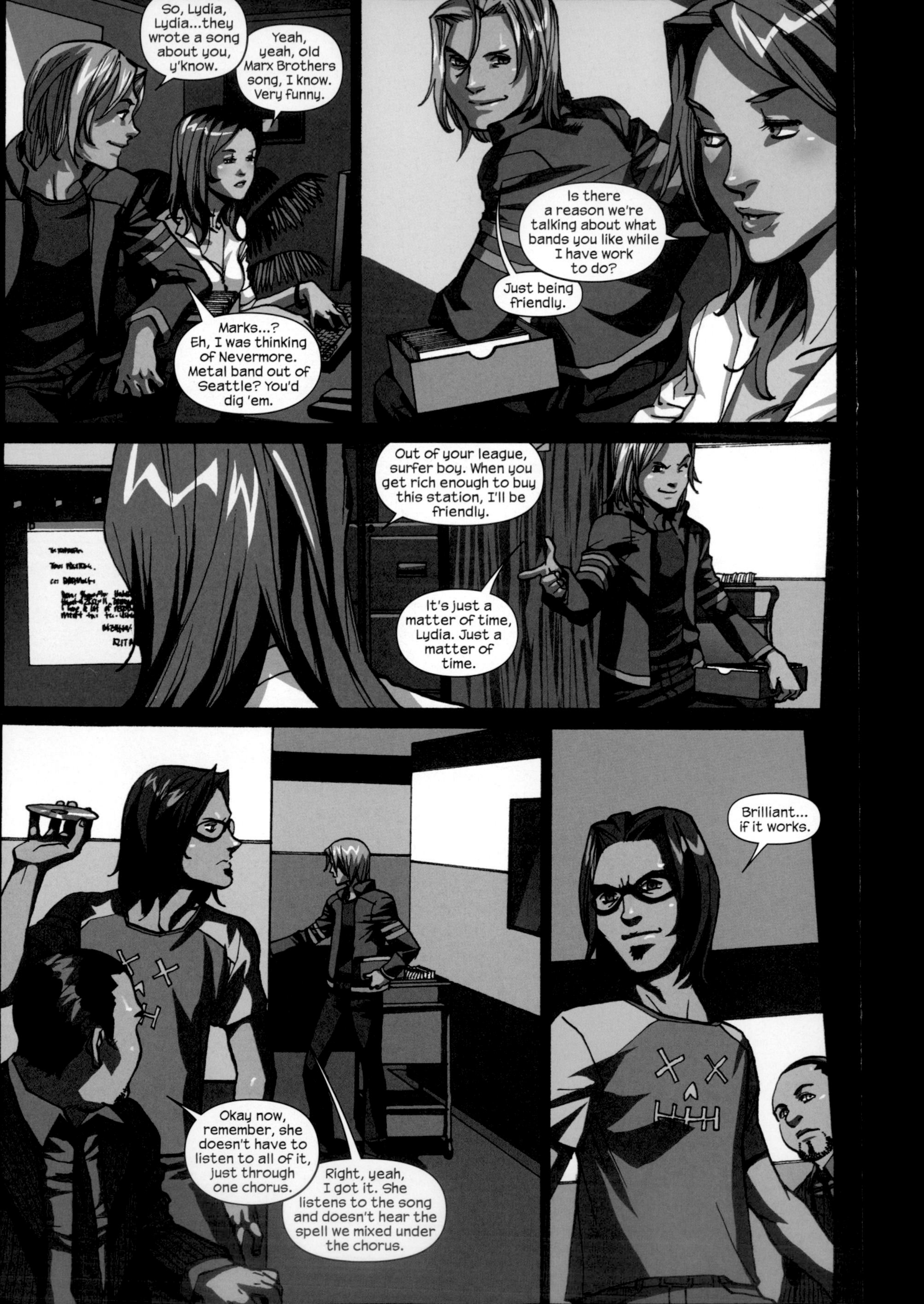
So, Lydia, Lydia...they wrote a song about you, y'know.
Yeah, yeah, old Marx Brothers song, I know. Very funny.
Marks...? Eh, I was thinking of Nevermore. Metal band out of Seattle? You'd dig 'em.
Is there a reason we're talking about what bands you like while I have work to do?
Just being friendly.
Out of your league, surfer boy. When you get rich enough to buy this station, I'll be friendly.
It's just a matter of time, Lydia. Just a matter of time.
Okay now, remember, she doesn't have to listen to all of it, just through one chorus.
Right, yeah, I got it. She listens to the song and doesn't hear the spell we mixed under the chorus.
Brilliant... if it works.

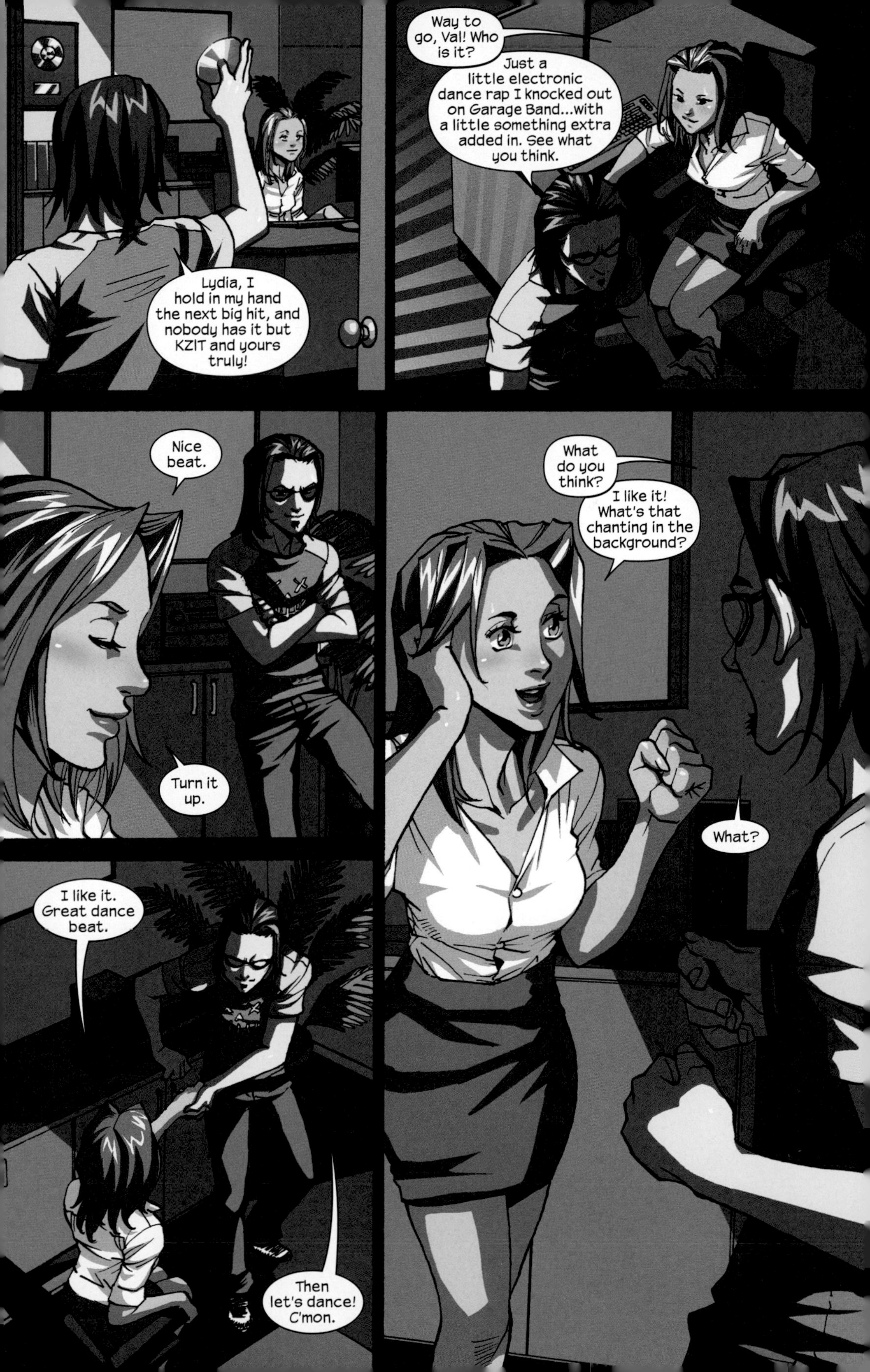
Lydia, I hold in my hand the next big hit, and nobody has it but KZIT and yours truly!
Way to go, Val! Who is it?
Just a little electronic dance rap I knocked out on Garage Band...with a little something extra added in. See what you think.
Nice beat.
Turn it up.
I like it. Great dance beat.
Then let's dance! C'mon.
What do you think?
I like it! What's that chanting in the background?
What?

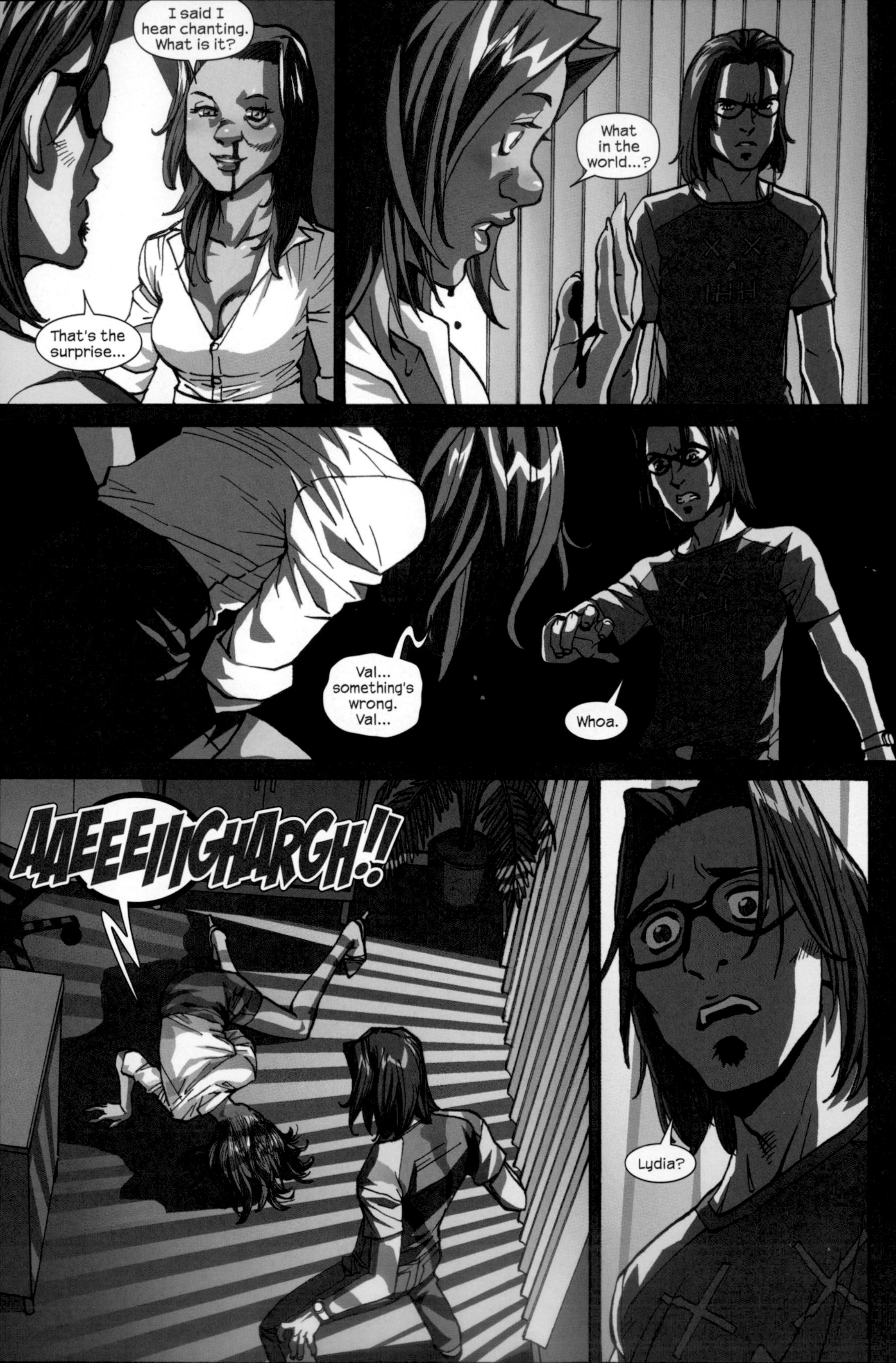
I said I hear chanting. What is it?
That's the surprise...
What in the world...?
Val... something's wrong. Val...
Whoa.
AAEEEIIIGHARGH!!
Lydia?

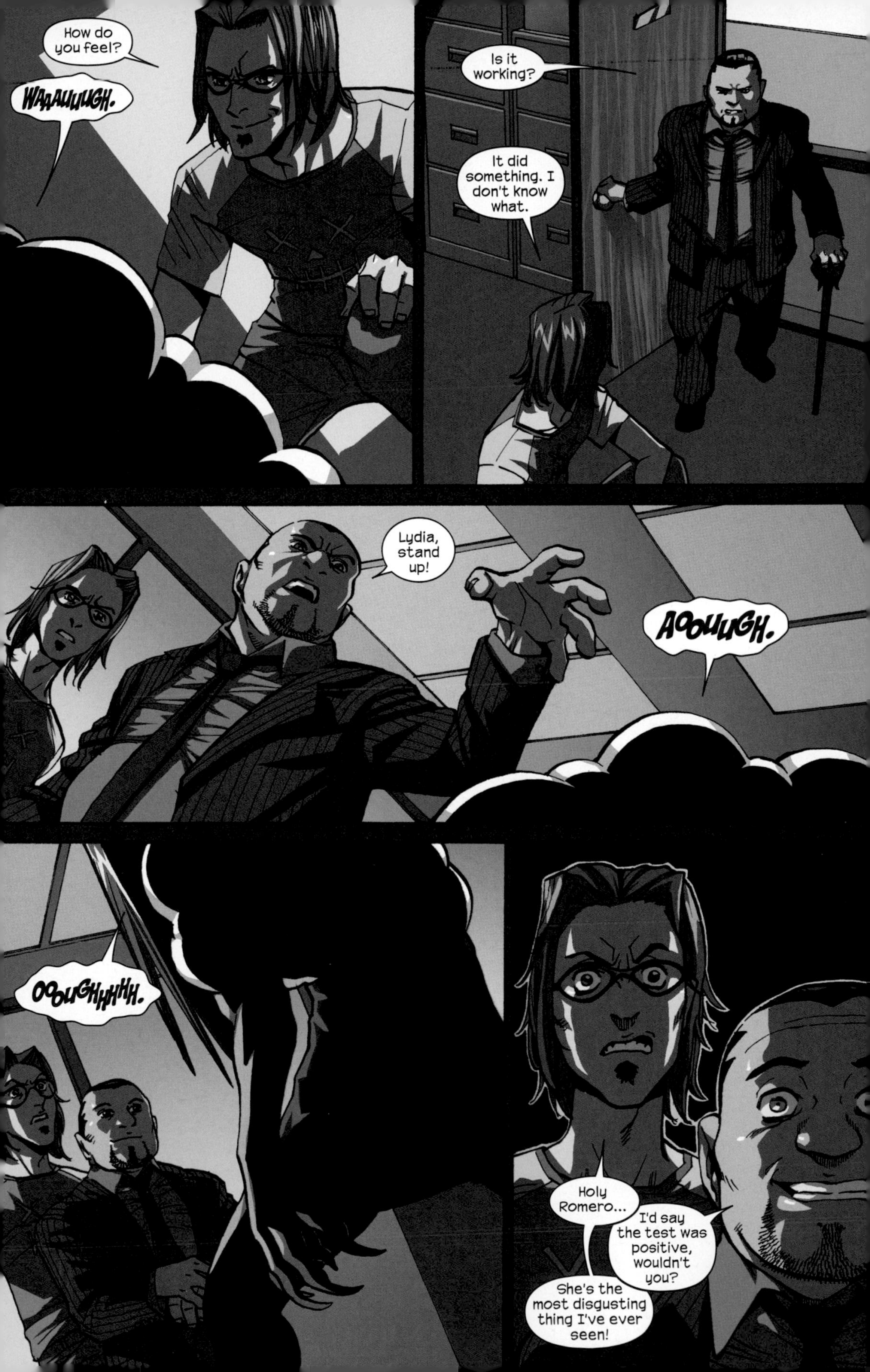
How do you feel?
WAAAUUUGH.
Is it working?
It did something. I don't know what.
Lydia, stand up!
AOOUUGH.
OOUGHHHHH.
Holy Romero...
I'd say the test was positive, wouldn't you?
She's the most disgusting thing I've ever seen!

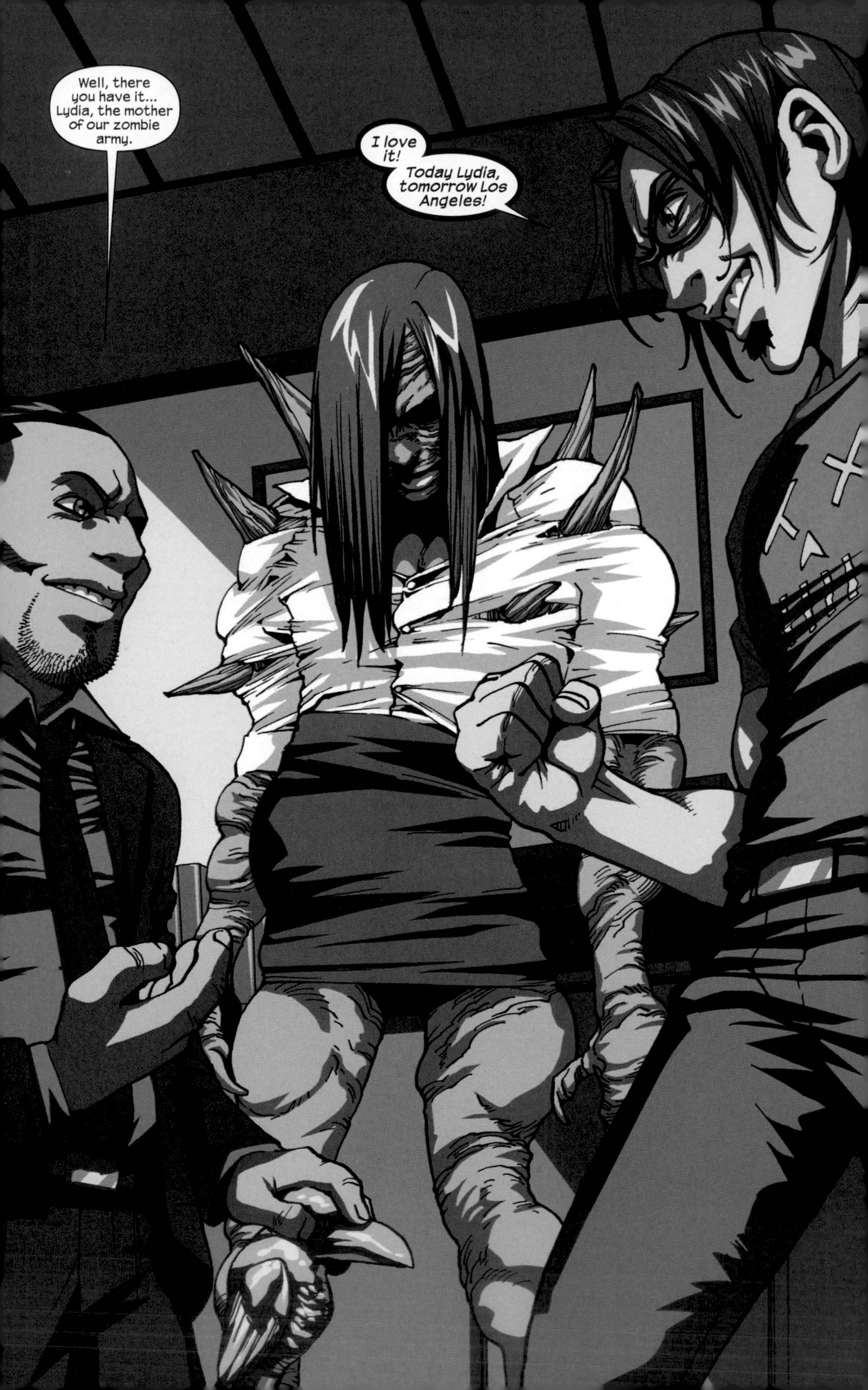
Well, there you have it... Lydia, the mother of our zombie army.
I love it!
Today Lydia, tomorrow Los Angeles!

8

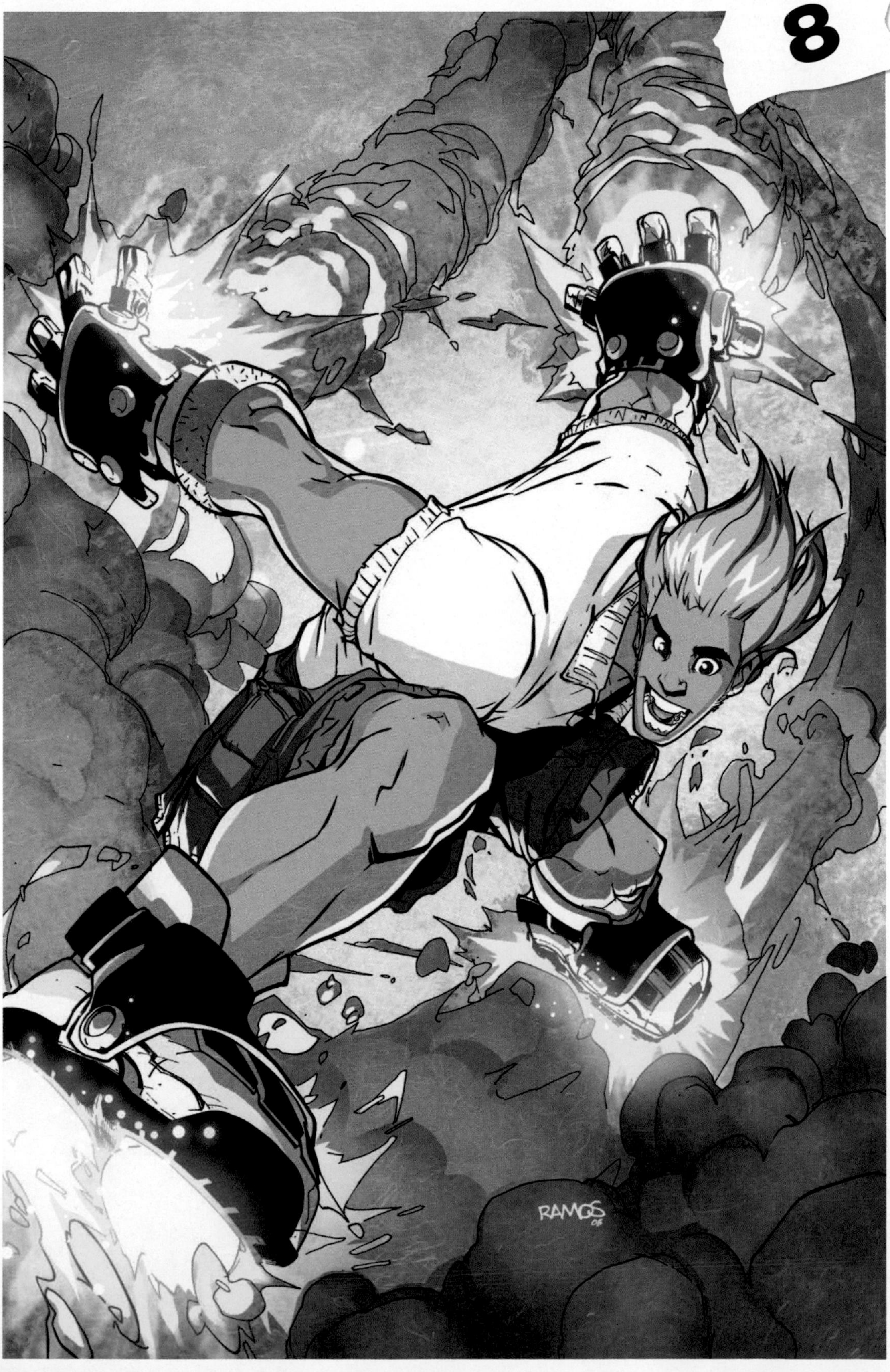
RAMOS

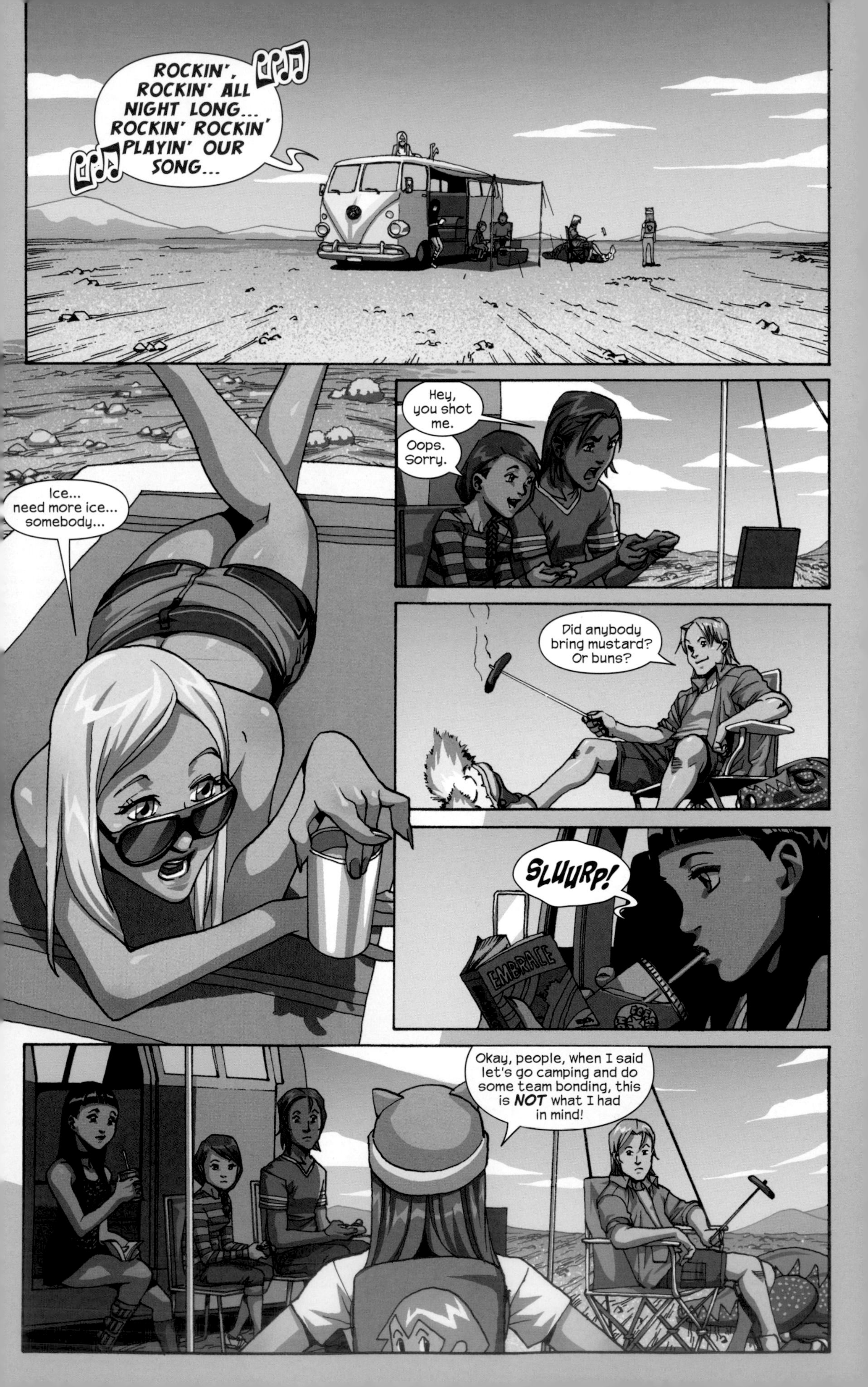
ROCKIN', ROCKIN' ALL NIGHT LONG... ROCKIN' ROCKIN' PLAYIN' OUR SONG...
Ice... need more ice... somebody...
Hey, you shot me.
Oops. Sorry.
Did anybody bring mustard? Or buns?
SLUURP!
EMBRACE
Okay, people, when I said let's go camping and do some team bonding, this is NOT what I had in mind!

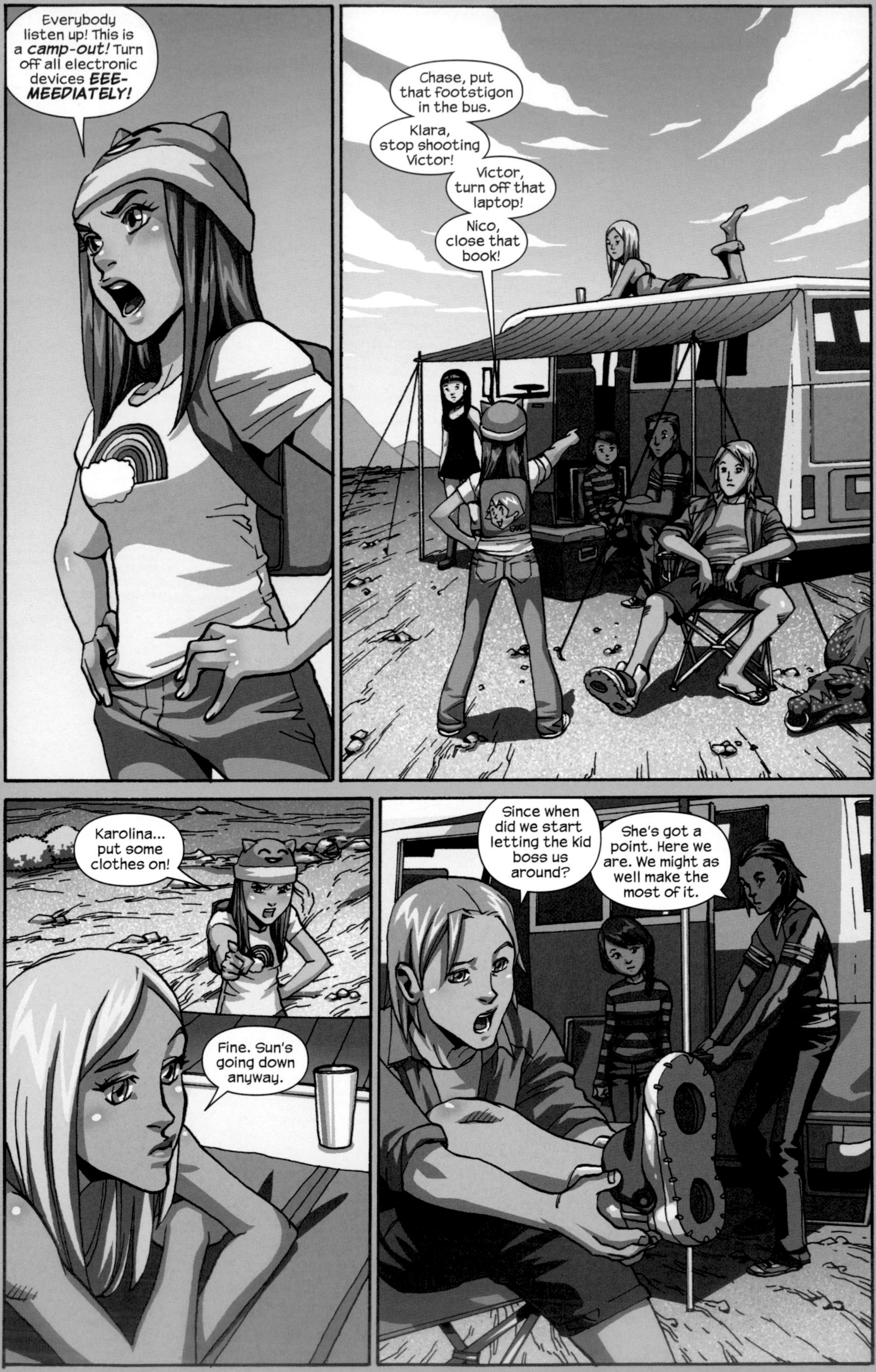
Everybody listen up! This is a *camp-out!* Turn off all electronic devices **EEE-MEEDIATELY!**
Chase, put that footstigon in the bus.
Klara, stop shooting Victor!
Victor, turn off that laptop!
Nico, close that book!
Karolina... put some clothes on!
Fine. Sun's going down anyway.
Since when did we start letting the kid boss us around?
She's got a point. Here we are. We might as well make the most of it.

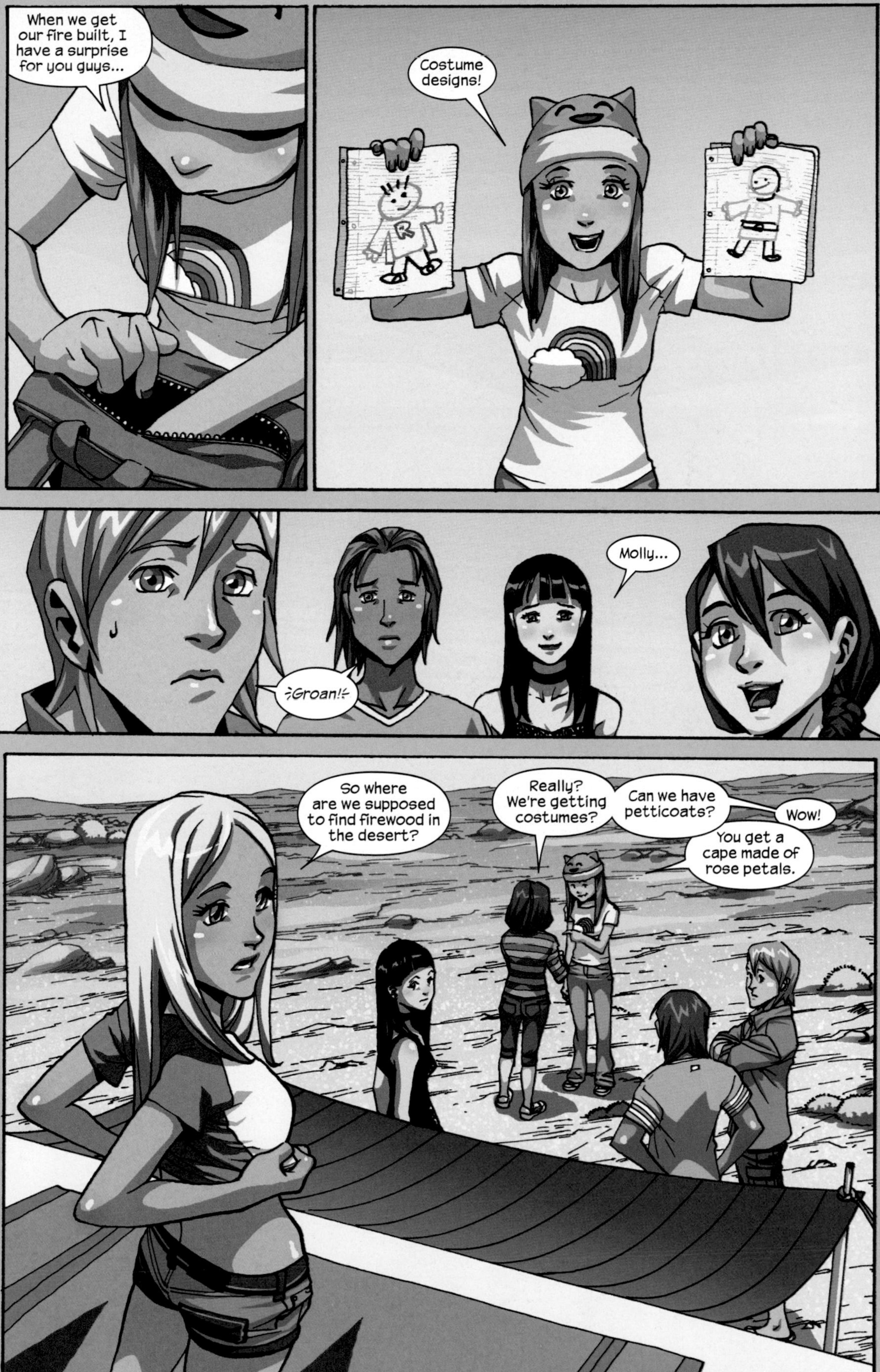
When we get our fire built, I have a surprise for you guys...
Costume designs!
R
Molly...
Groan!
So where are we supposed to find firewood in the desert?
Really? We're getting costumes?
Can we have petticoats?
Wow!
You get a cape made of rose petals.

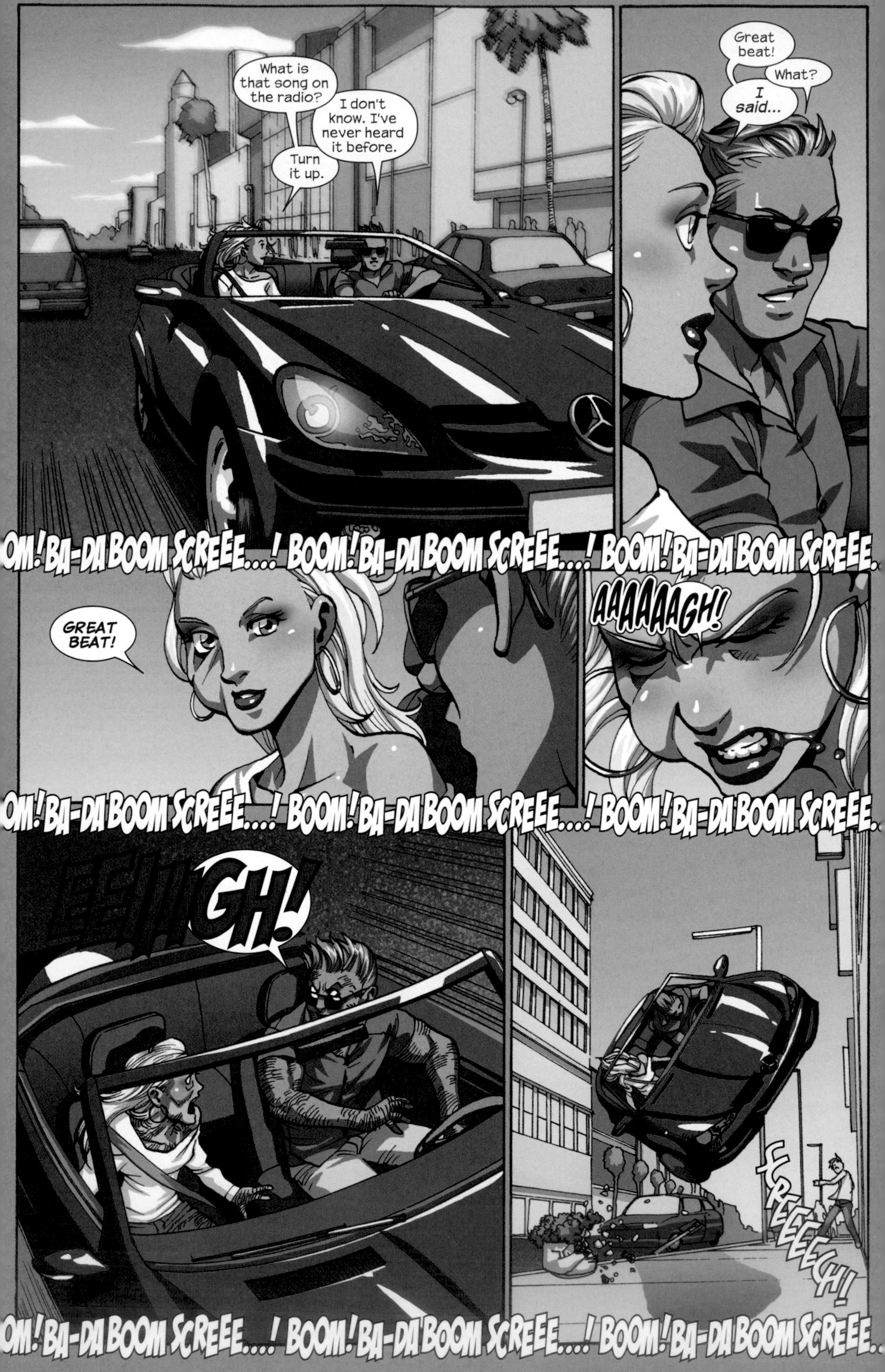
What is that song on the radio?
I don't know. I've never heard it before.
Turn it up.
Great beat!
What?
I said...
OM! BA-DA BOOM SCREEE...! BOOM! BA-DA BOOM SCREEE...! BOOM! BA-DA BOOM SCREEE.
GREAT BEAT!
AAAAAAGH!
OM! BA-DA BOOM SCREEE...! BOOM! BA-DA BOOM SCREEE...! BOOM! BA-DA BOOM SCREEE.
EEIIIGH!
SCREEEECH!
OM! BA-DA BOOM SCREEE...! BOOM! BA-DA BOOM SCREEE...! BOOM! BA-DA BOOM SCREEE.

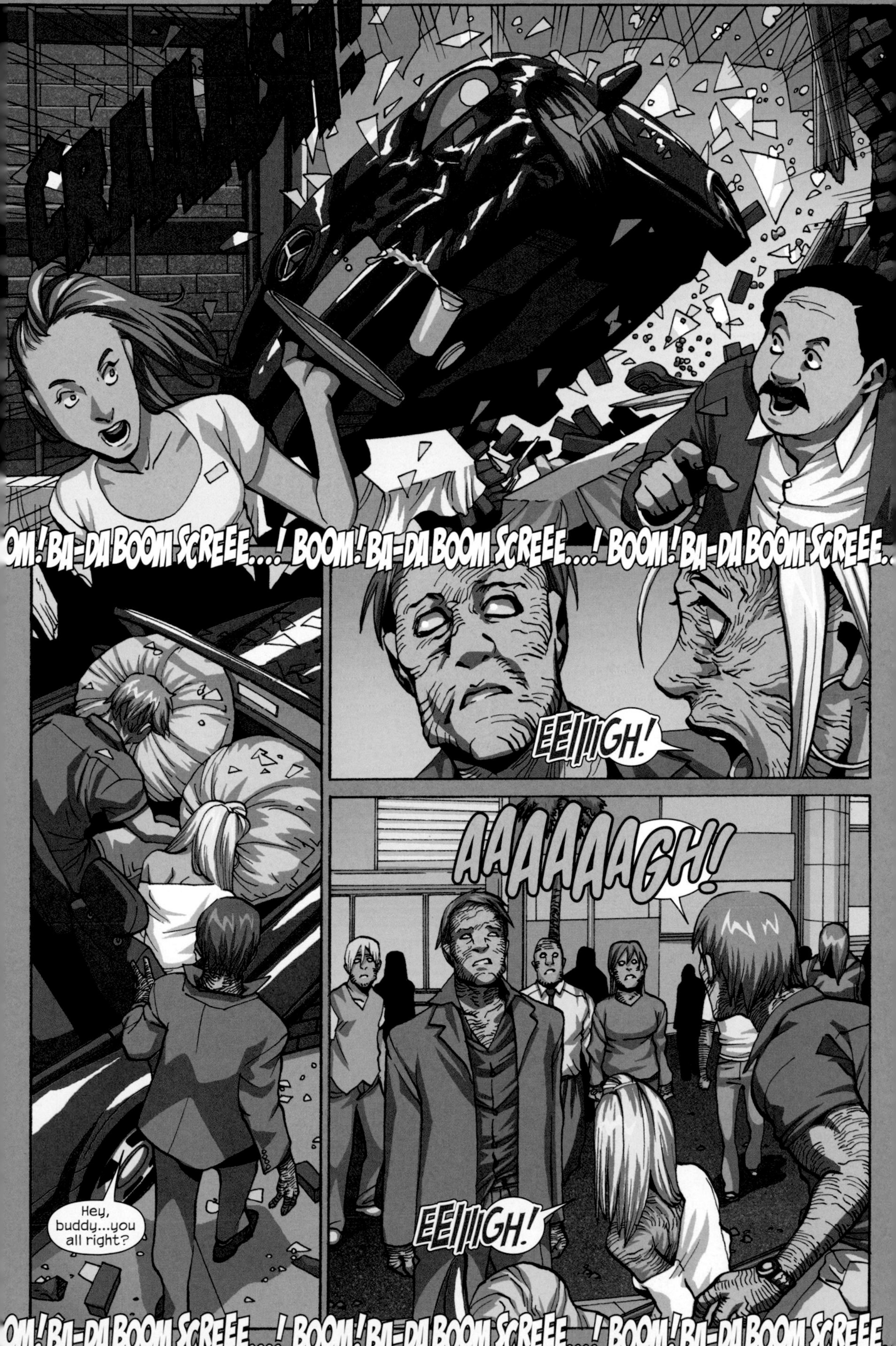
CRAAAASH!!
OM! BA-DA BOOM SCREEE...! BOOM! BA-DA BOOM SCREEE...! BOOM! BA-DA BOOM SCREEE..
EEIIIIGH!
Hey, buddy...you all right?
AAAAAAAGH!
EEIIIIGH!
OM! BA-DA BOOM SCREEE...! BOOM! BA-DA BOOM SCREEE...! BOOM! BA-DA BOOM SCREEE..

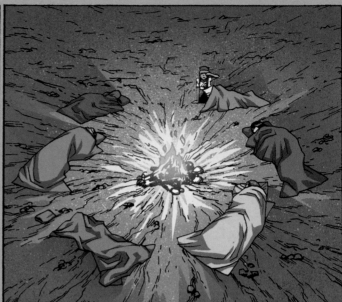

Mornin'.

Hey, K.

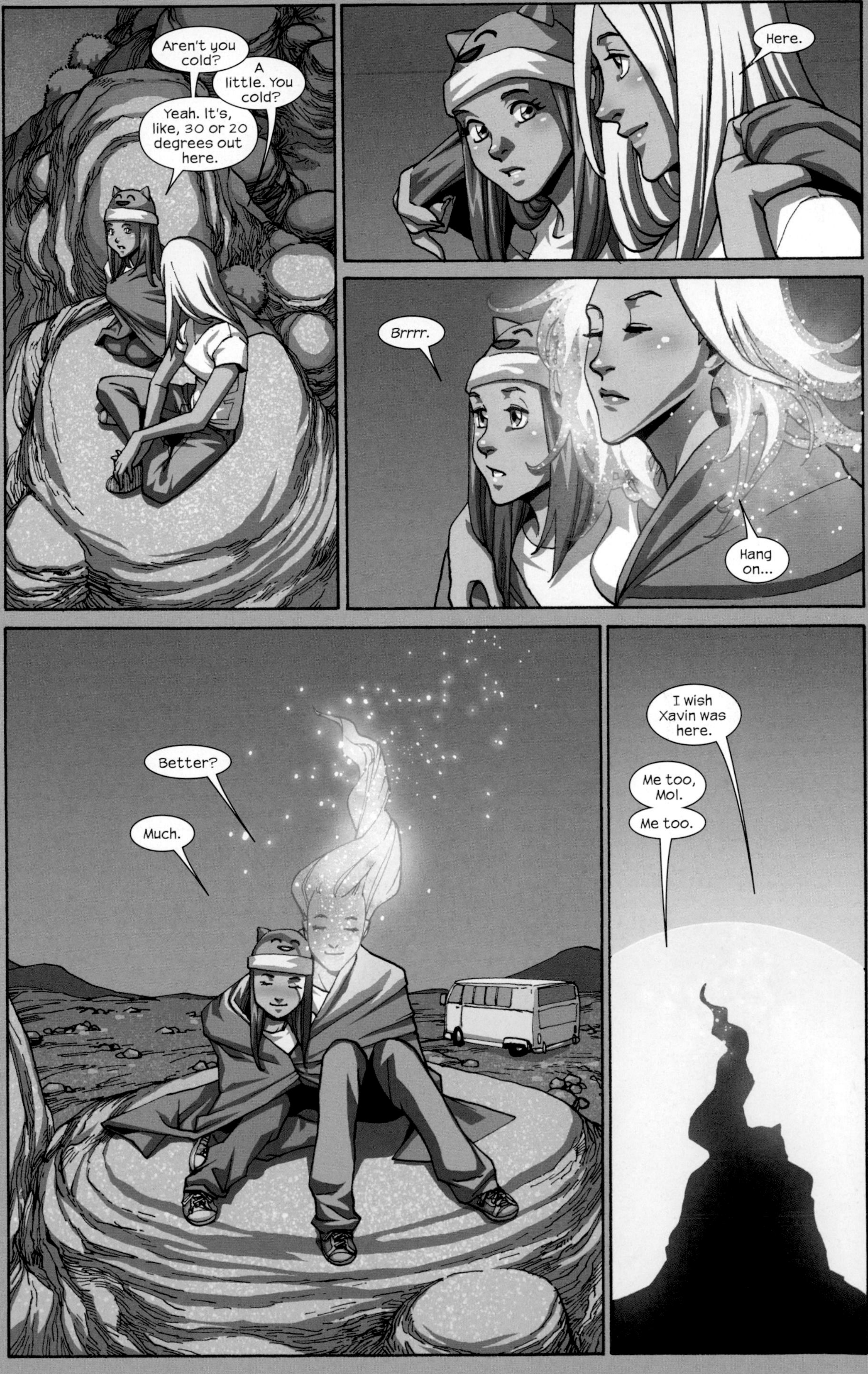
Aren't you cold?
A little. You cold?
Yeah. It's, like, 30 or 20 degrees out here.
Here.
Brrrr.
Hang on...
Better?
Much.
I wish Xavin was here.
Me too, Mol.
Me too.

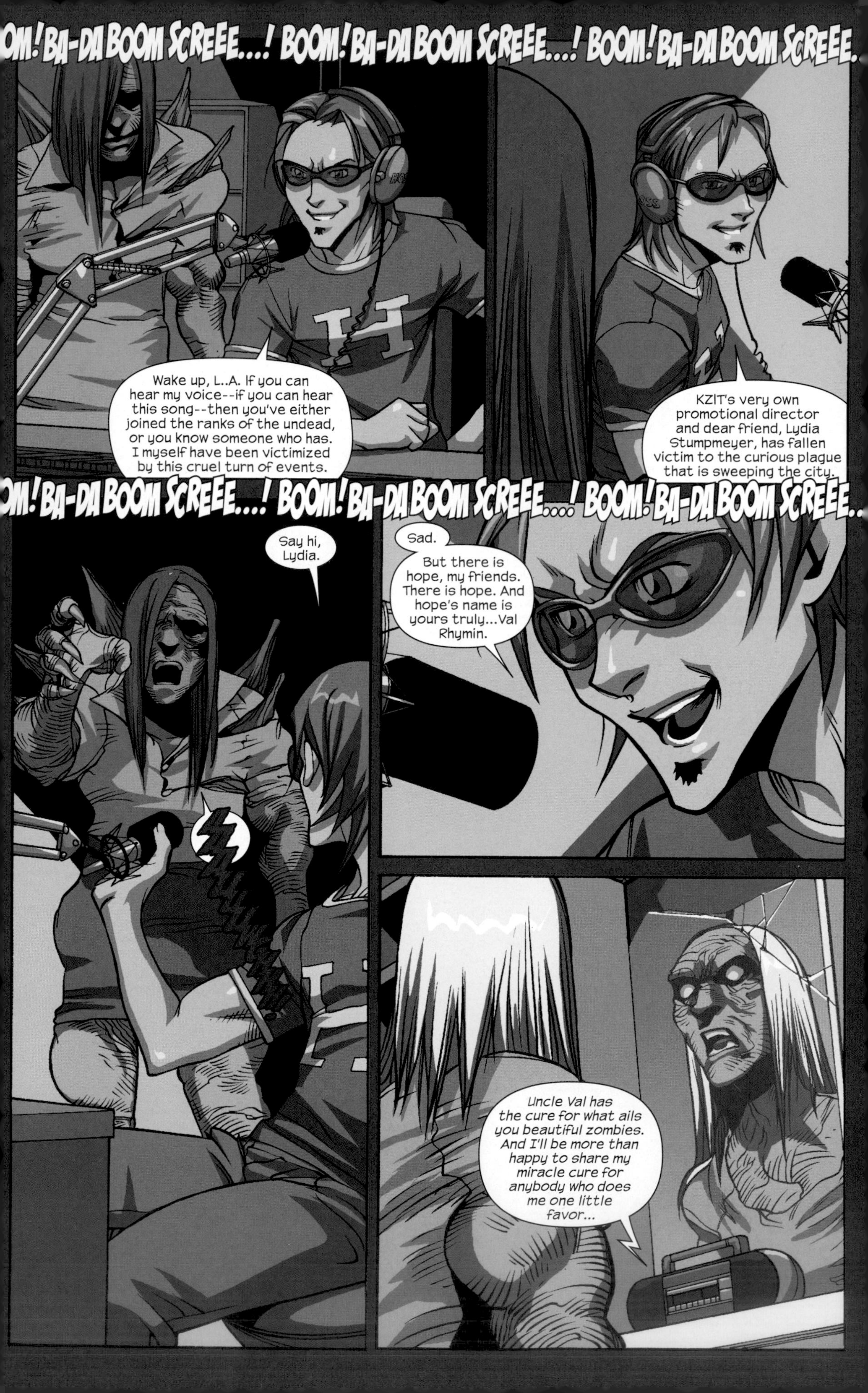
OM! BA-DA BOOM SCREEE...! BOOM! BA-DA BOOM SCREEE...! BOOM! BA-DA BOOM SCREEE...
Wake up, L..A. If you can hear my voice--if you can hear this song--then you've either joined the ranks of the undead, or you know someone who has. I myself have been victimized by this cruel turn of events.
KZIT's very own promotional director and dear friend, Lydia Stumpmeyer, has fallen victim to the curious plague that is sweeping the city.
OM! BA-DA BOOM SCREEE...! BOOM! BA-DA BOOM SCREEE...! BOOM! BA-DA BOOM SCREEE...
Say hi, Lydia.
Sad.
But there is hope, my friends. There is hope. And hope's name is yours truly...Val Rhymin.
Uncle Val has the cure for what ails you beautiful zombies. And I'll be more than happy to share my miracle cure for anybody who does me one little favor...

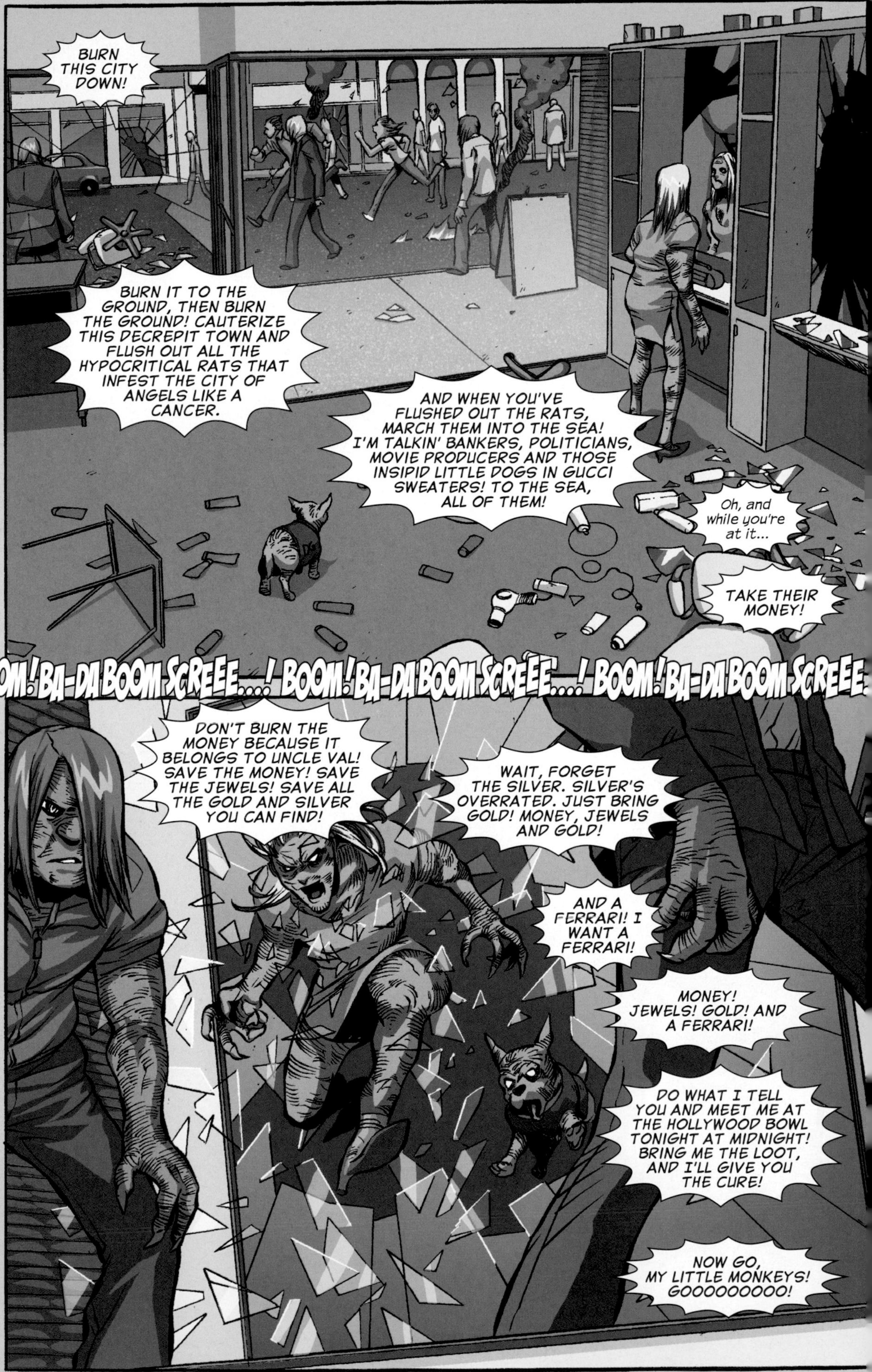
BURN THIS CITY DOWN!
BURN IT TO THE GROUND, THEN BURN THE GROUND! CAUTERIZE THIS DECREPIT TOWN AND FLUSH OUT ALL THE HYPOCRITICAL RATS THAT INFEST THE CITY OF ANGELS LIKE A CANCER.
AND WHEN YOU'VE FLUSHED OUT THE RATS, MARCH THEM INTO THE SEA! I'M TALKIN' BANKERS, POLITICIANS, MOVIE PRODUCERS AND THOSE INSIPID LITTLE DOGS IN GUCCI SWEATERS! TO THE SEA, ALL OF THEM!
Oh, and while you're at it...
TAKE THEIR MONEY!
OOM! BA-DA BOOM SCREEE...! BOOM! BA-DA BOOM SCREEE...! BOOM! BA-DA BOOM SCREEE.
DON'T BURN THE MONEY BECAUSE IT BELONGS TO UNCLE VAL! SAVE THE MONEY! SAVE THE JEWELS! SAVE ALL THE GOLD AND SILVER YOU CAN FIND!
WAIT, FORGET THE SILVER. SILVER'S OVERRATED. JUST BRING GOLD! MONEY, JEWELS AND GOLD!
AND A FERRARI! I WANT A FERRARI!
MONEY! JEWELS! GOLD! AND A FERRARI!
DO WHAT I TELL YOU AND MEET ME AT THE HOLLYWOOD BOWL TONIGHT AT MIDNIGHT! BRING ME THE LOOT, AND I'LL GIVE YOU THE CURE!
NOW GO, MY LITTLE MONKEYS! GOOOOOOOOO!

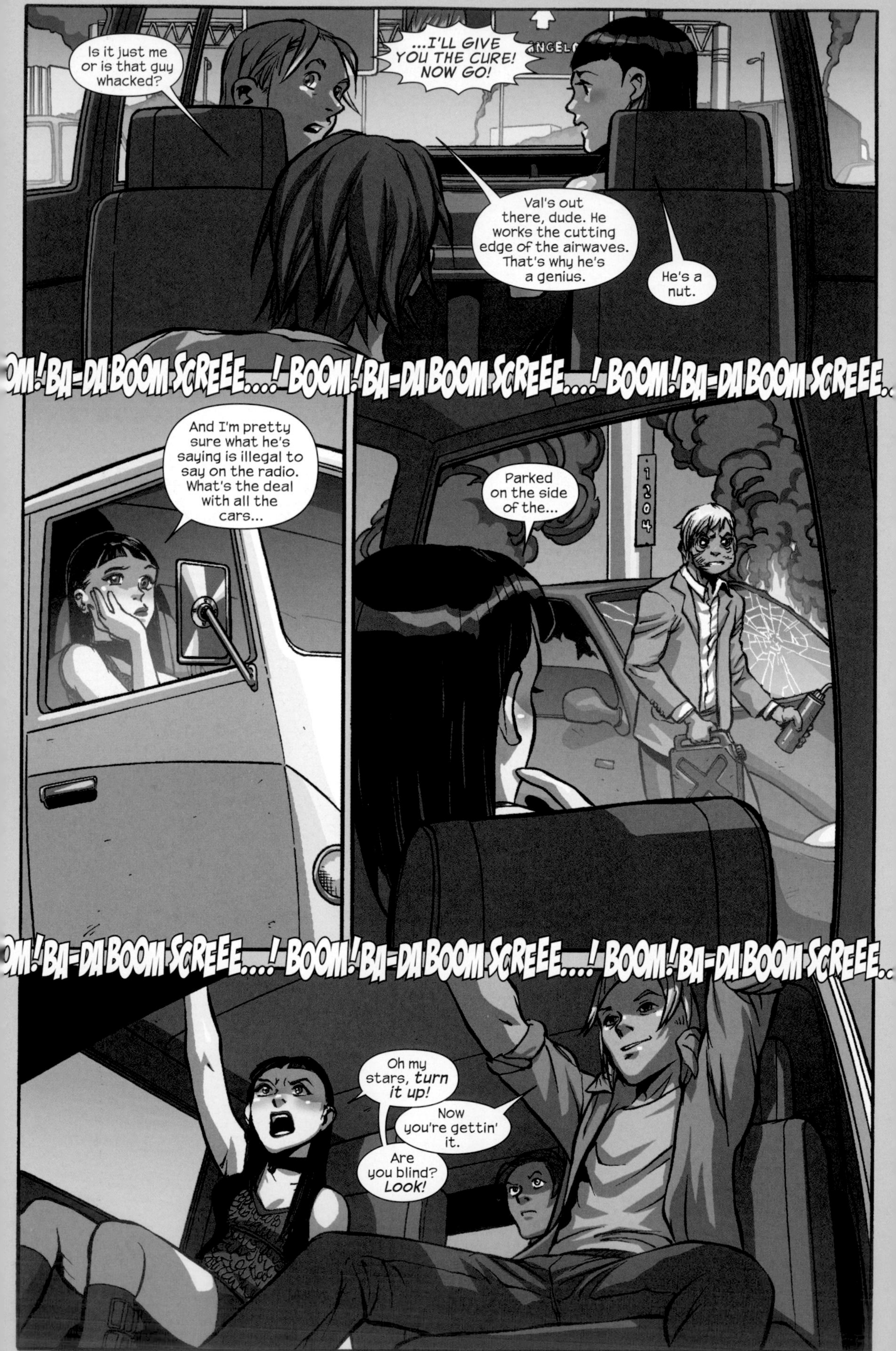

Is it just me or is that guy whacked?
...I'LL GIVE YOU THE CURE! NOW GO!
ANGELO
Val's out there, dude. He works the cutting edge of the airwaves. That's why he's a genius.
He's a nut.
BOOM! BA-DA BOOM SCREEE...! BOOM! BA-DA BOOM SCREEE...! BOOM! BA-DA BOOM SCREEE..
And I'm pretty sure what he's saying is illegal to say on the radio. What's the deal with all the cars...
Parked on the side of the...
1204
BOOM! BA-DA BOOM SCREEE...! BOOM! BA-DA BOOM SCREEE...! BOOM! BA-DA BOOM SCREEE..
Oh my stars, *turn it up!*
Now you're gettin' it.
Are you blind? *LOOK!*

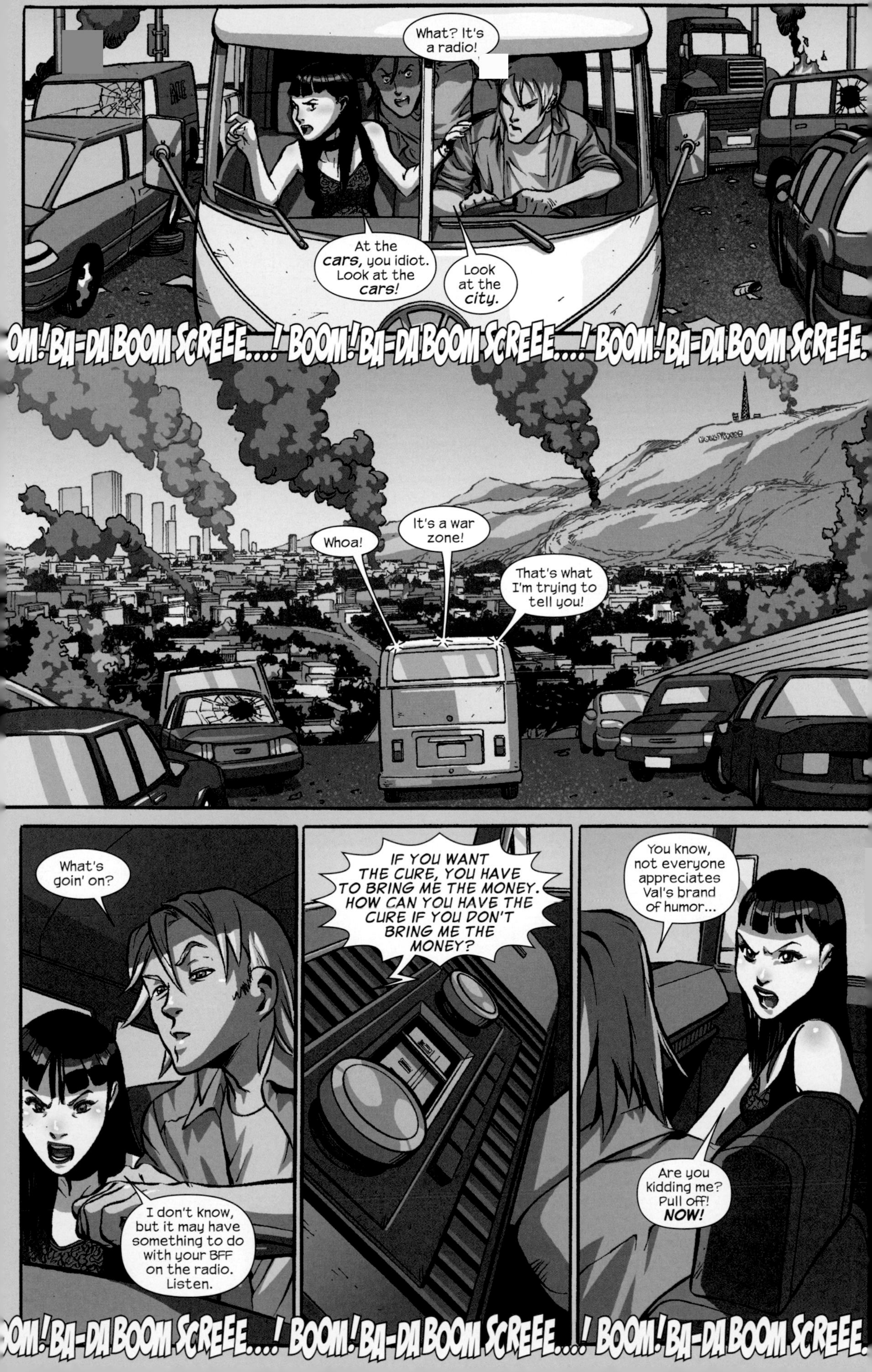

What? It's a radio!
At the cars, you idiot. Look at the cars!
Look at the city.
OM! BA-DA BOOM SCREEE...! BOOM! BA-DA BOOM SCREEE...! BOOM! BA-DA BOOM SCREEE.
Whoa!
It's a war zone!
That's what I'm trying to tell you!
What's goin' on?
I don't know, but it may have something to do with your BFF on the radio. Listen.
IF YOU WANT THE CURE, YOU HAVE TO BRING ME THE MONEY. HOW CAN YOU HAVE THE CURE IF YOU DON'T BRING ME THE MONEY?
You know, not everyone appreciates Val's brand of humor...
Are you kidding me? Pull off! NOW!
OM! BA-DA BOOM SCREEE...! BOOM! BA-DA BOOM SCREEE...! BOOM! BA-DA BOOM SCREEE.

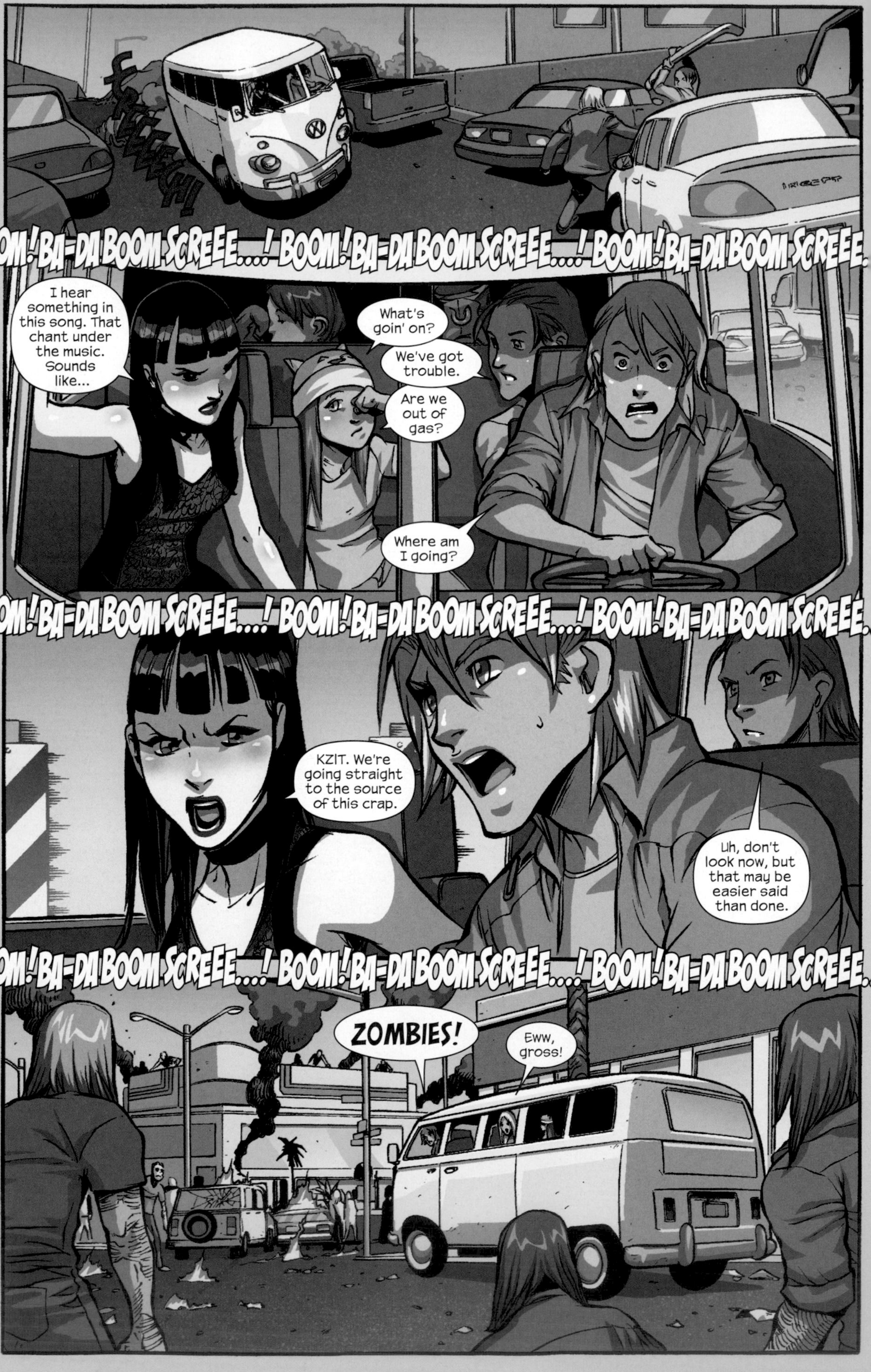
OM! BA-DA BOOM SCREEE...! BOOM! BA-DA BOOM SCREEE...! BOOM! BA-DA BOOM SCREEE.
I hear something in this song. That chant under the music. Sounds like...
What's goin' on?
We've got trouble.
Are we out of gas?
Where am I going?
OM! BA-DA BOOM SCREEE...! BOOM! BA-DA BOOM SCREEE...! BOOM! BA-DA BOOM SCREEE.
KZIT. We're going straight to the source of this crap.
Uh, don't look now, but that may be easier said than done.
OM! BA-DA BOOM SCREEE...! BOOM! BA-DA BOOM SCREEE...! BOOM! BA-DA BOOM SCREEE.
ZOMBIES!
Eww, gross!

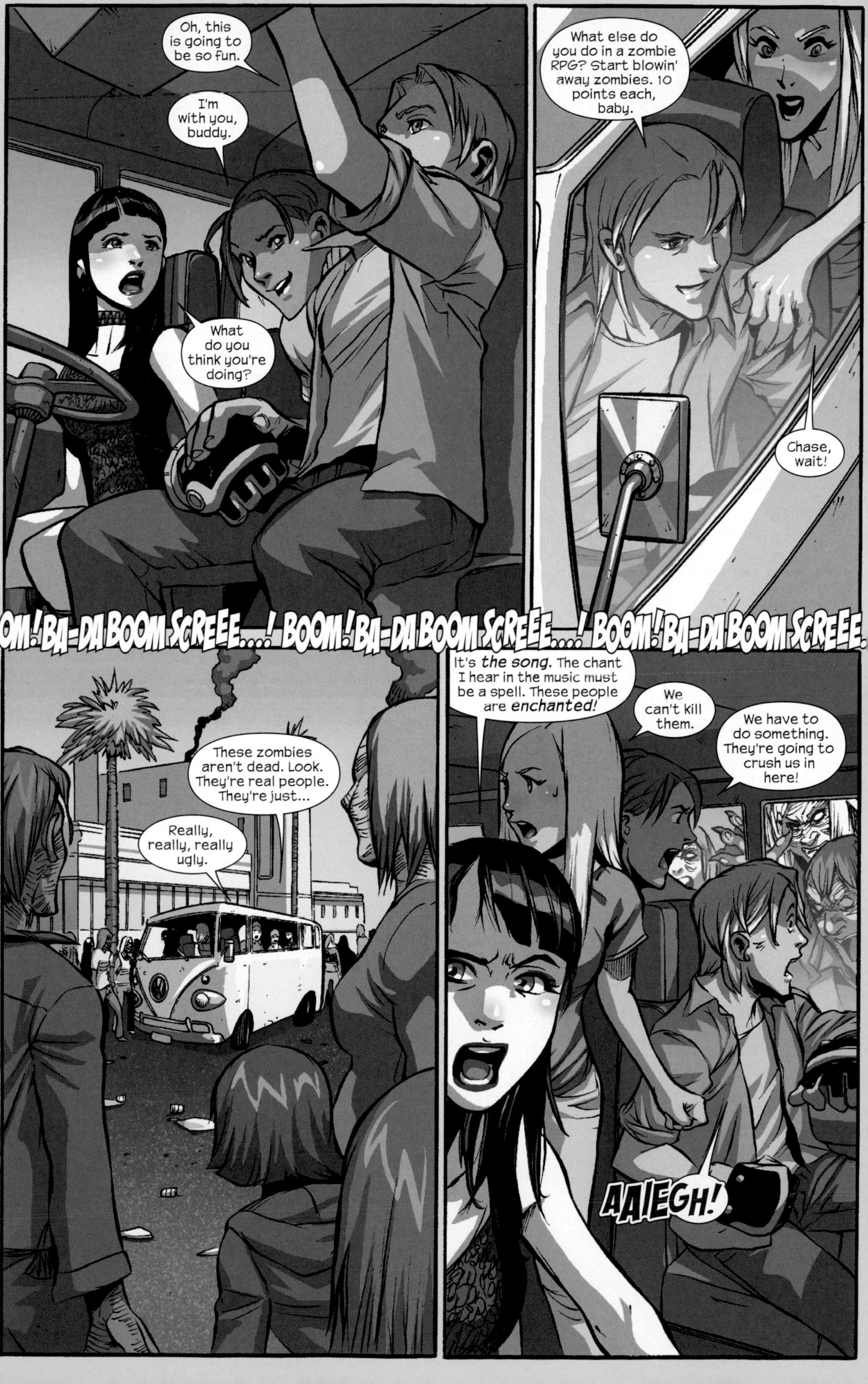
Oh, this is going to be so fun.
I'm with you, buddy.
What do you think you're doing?
What else do you do in a zombie RPG? Start blowin' away zombies. 10 points each, baby.
Chase, wait!
BOOM! BA-DA BOOM SCREEE...! BOOM! BA-DA BOOM SCREEE...! BOOM! BA-DA BOOM SCREEE.
These zombies aren't dead. Look. They're real people. They're just...
Really, really, really ugly.
It's *the song.* The chant I hear in the music must be a spell. These people are *enchanted!*
We can't kill them.
We have to do something. They're going to crush us in here!
AAIEGH!

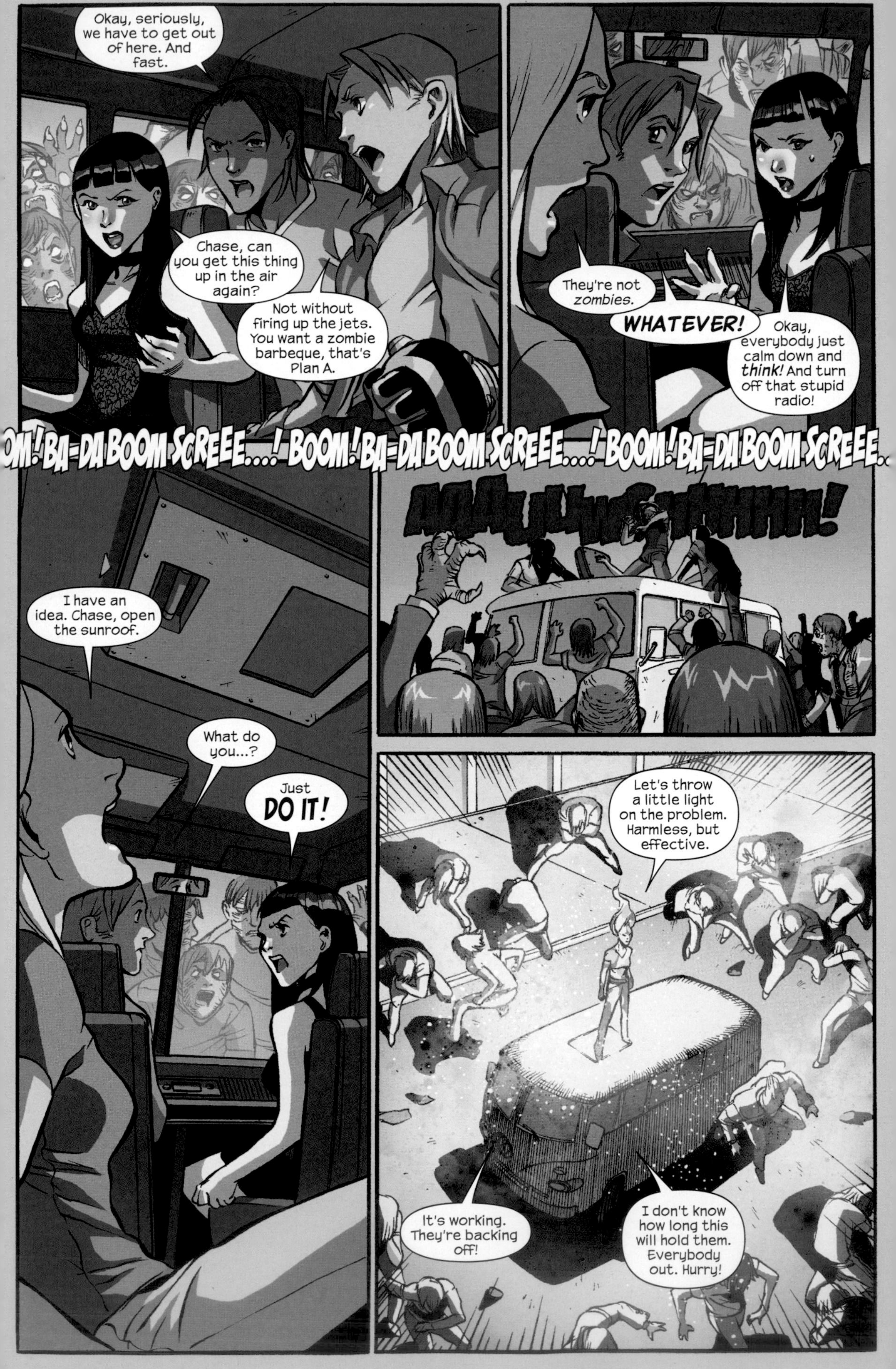

Okay, seriously, we have to get out of here. And fast.
Chase, can you get this thing up in the air again?
Not without firing up the jets. You want a zombie barbeque, that's Plan A.
They're not zombies.
WHATEVER!
Okay, everybody just calm down and *think!* And turn off that stupid radio!
OM! BA-DA BOOM SCREEE...! BOOM! BA-DA BOOM SCREEE...! BOOM! BA-DA BOOM SCREEE..
I have an idea. Chase, open the sunroof.
What do you...?
Just DO IT!
Let's throw a little light on the problem. Harmless, but effective.
It's working. They're backing off!
I don't know how long this will hold them. Everybody out. Hurry!

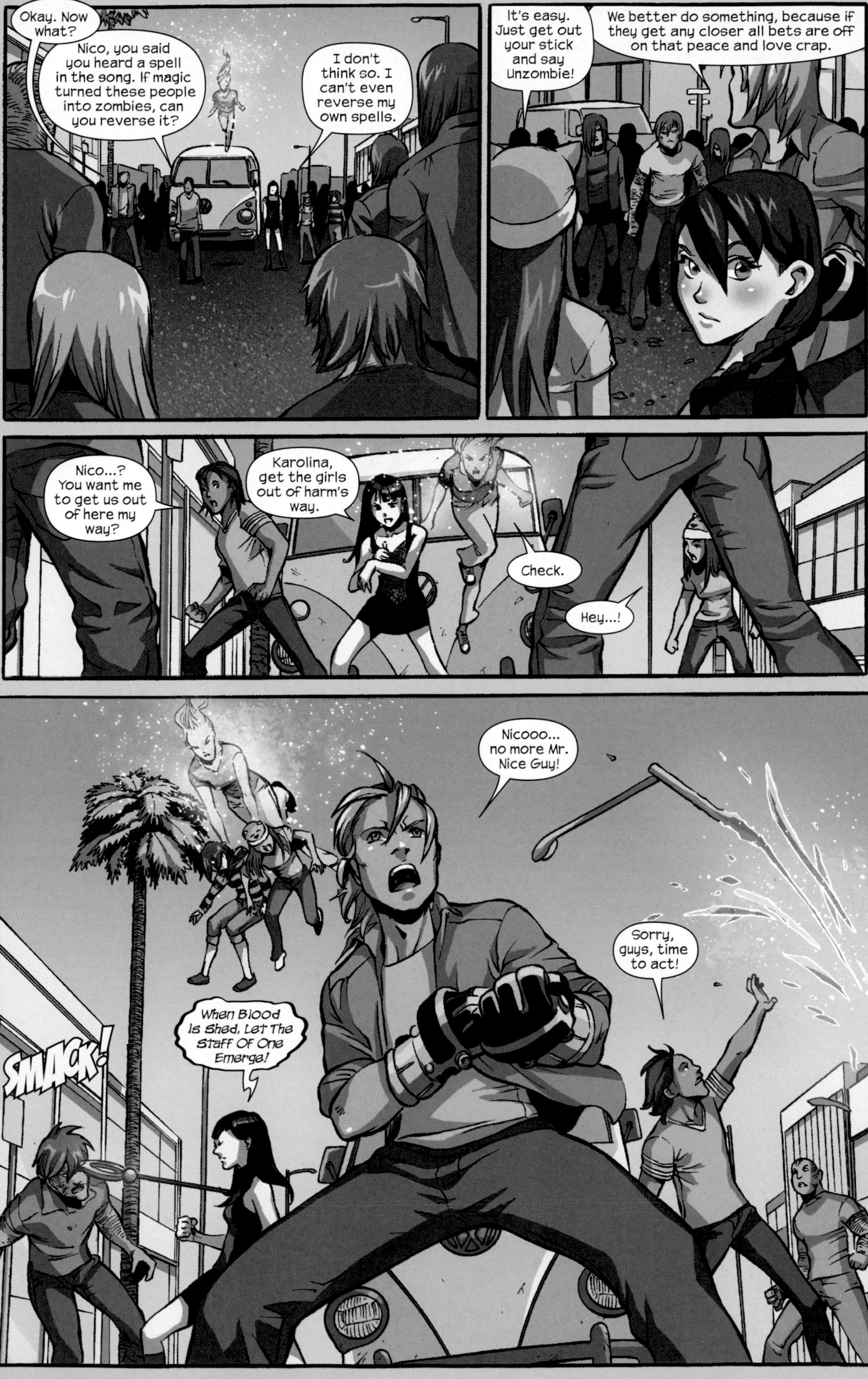
Okay. Now what?
Nico, you said you heard a spell in the song. If magic turned these people into zombies, can you reverse it?
I don't think so. I can't even reverse my own spells.
It's easy. Just get out your stick and say Unzombie!
We better do something, because if they get any closer all bets are off on that peace and love crap.
Nico...? You want me to get us out of here my way?
Karolina, get the girls out of harm's way.
Check.
Hey...!
Nicooo... no more Mr. Nice Guy!
When Blood Is Shed, Let The Staff Of One Emerge!
SMACK!
Sorry, guys, time to act!

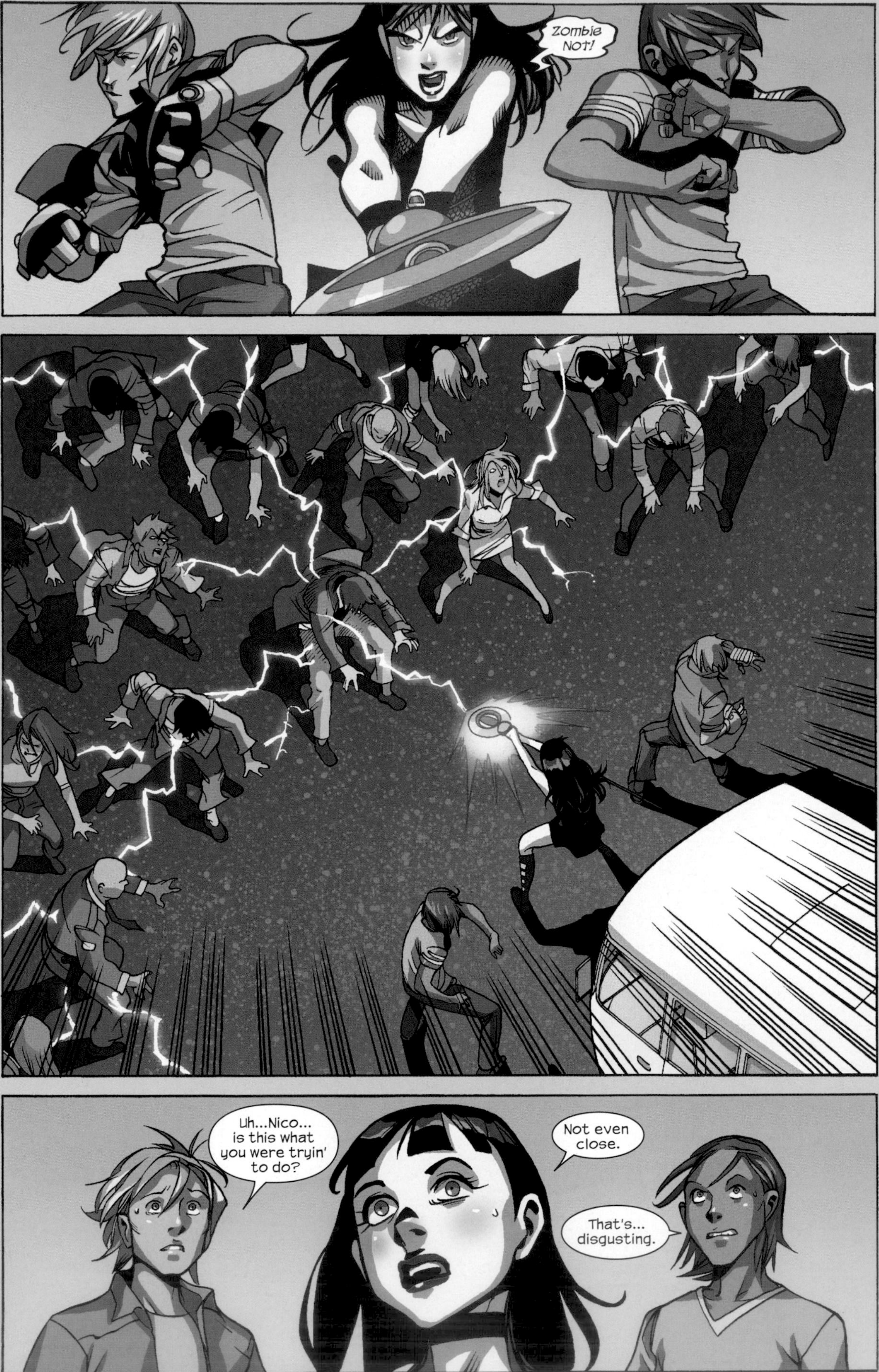
Zombie Not!
Uh...Nico... is this what you were tryin' to do?
Not even close.
That's... disgusting.

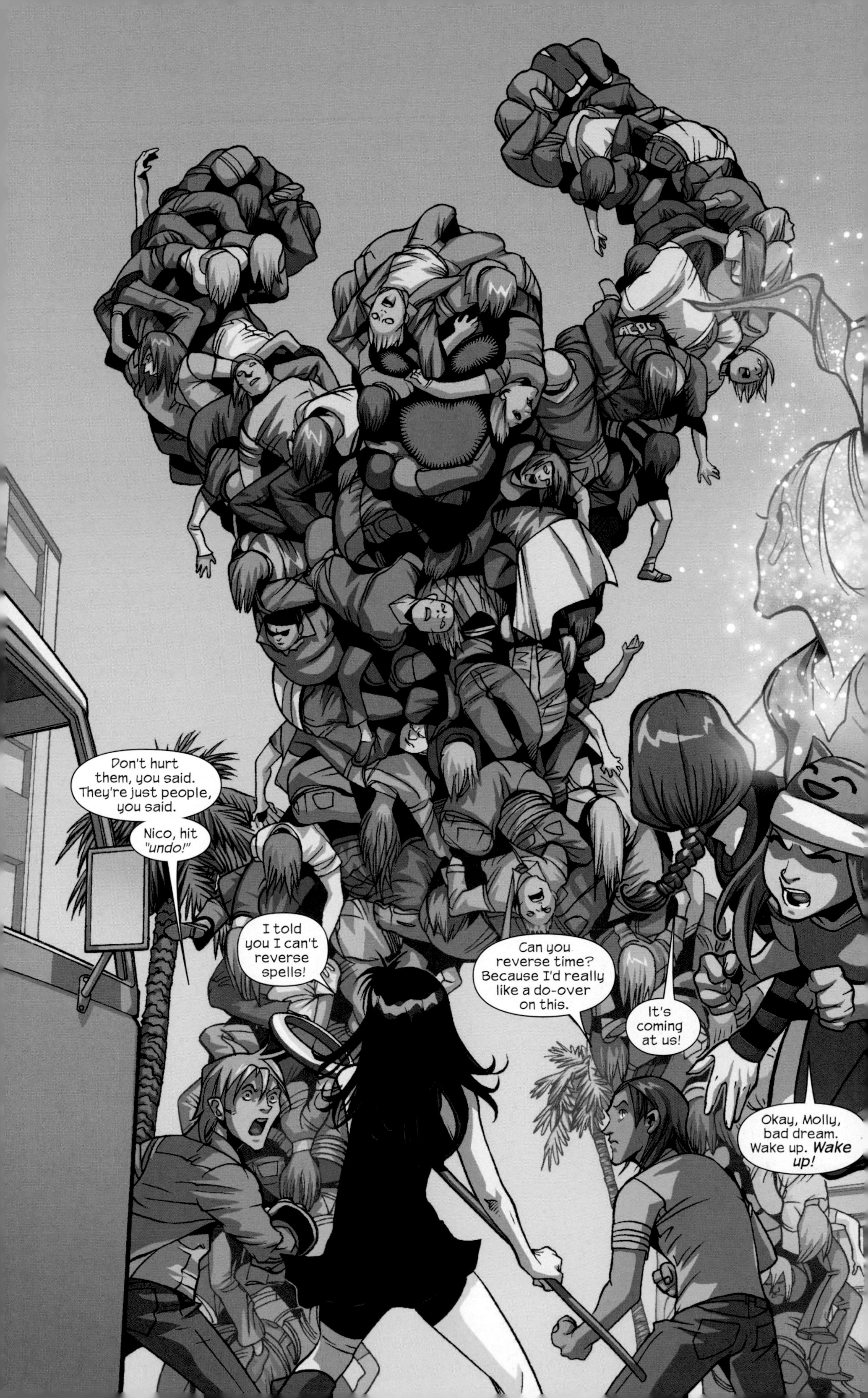
Don't hurt them, you said. They're just people, you said.
Nico, hit "undo!"
I told you I can't reverse spells!
Can you reverse time? Because I'd really like a do-over on this.
It's coming at us!
Okay, Molly, bad dream. Wake up. **Wake up!**

9

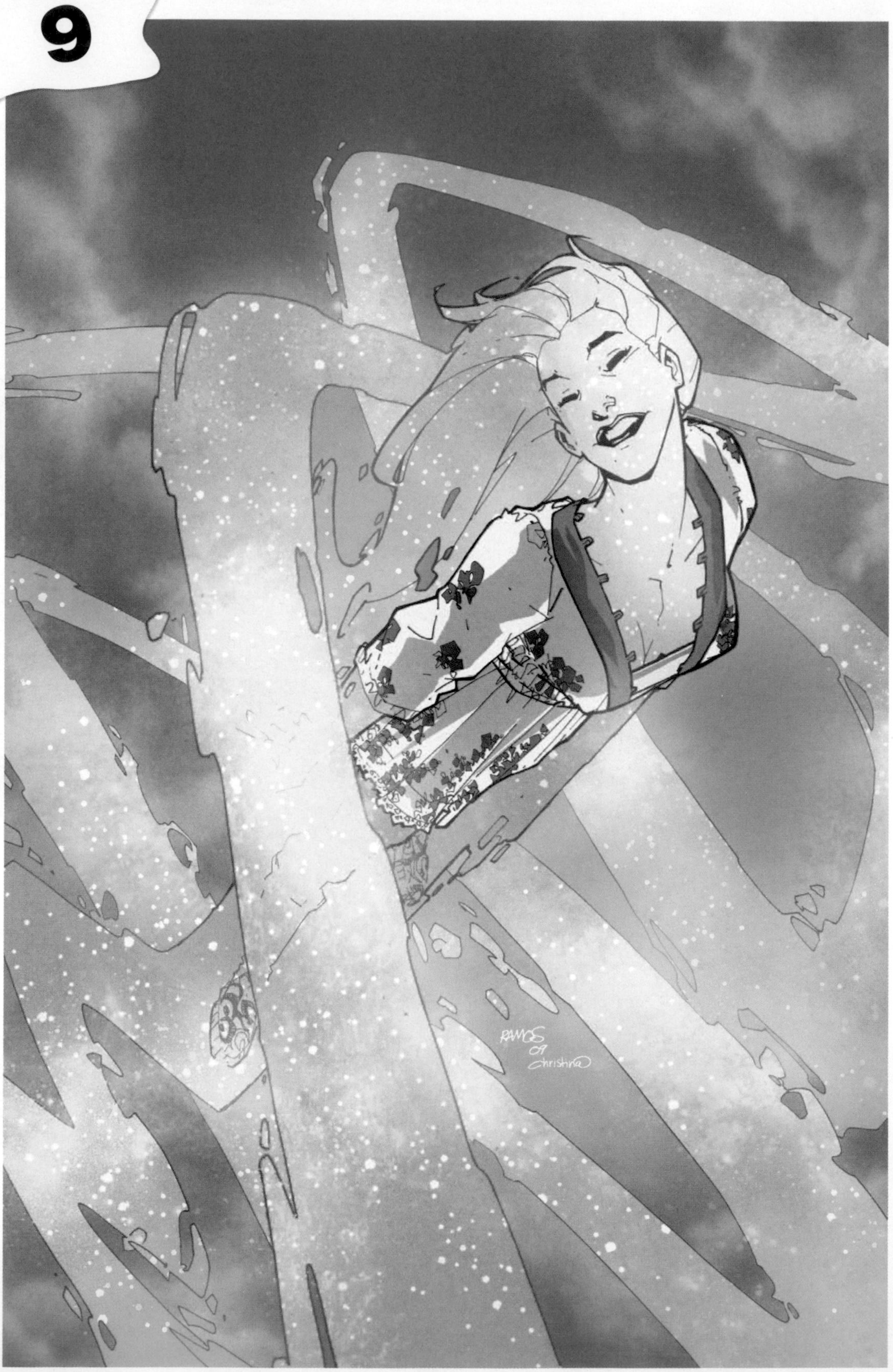
RAMOS
09
christina

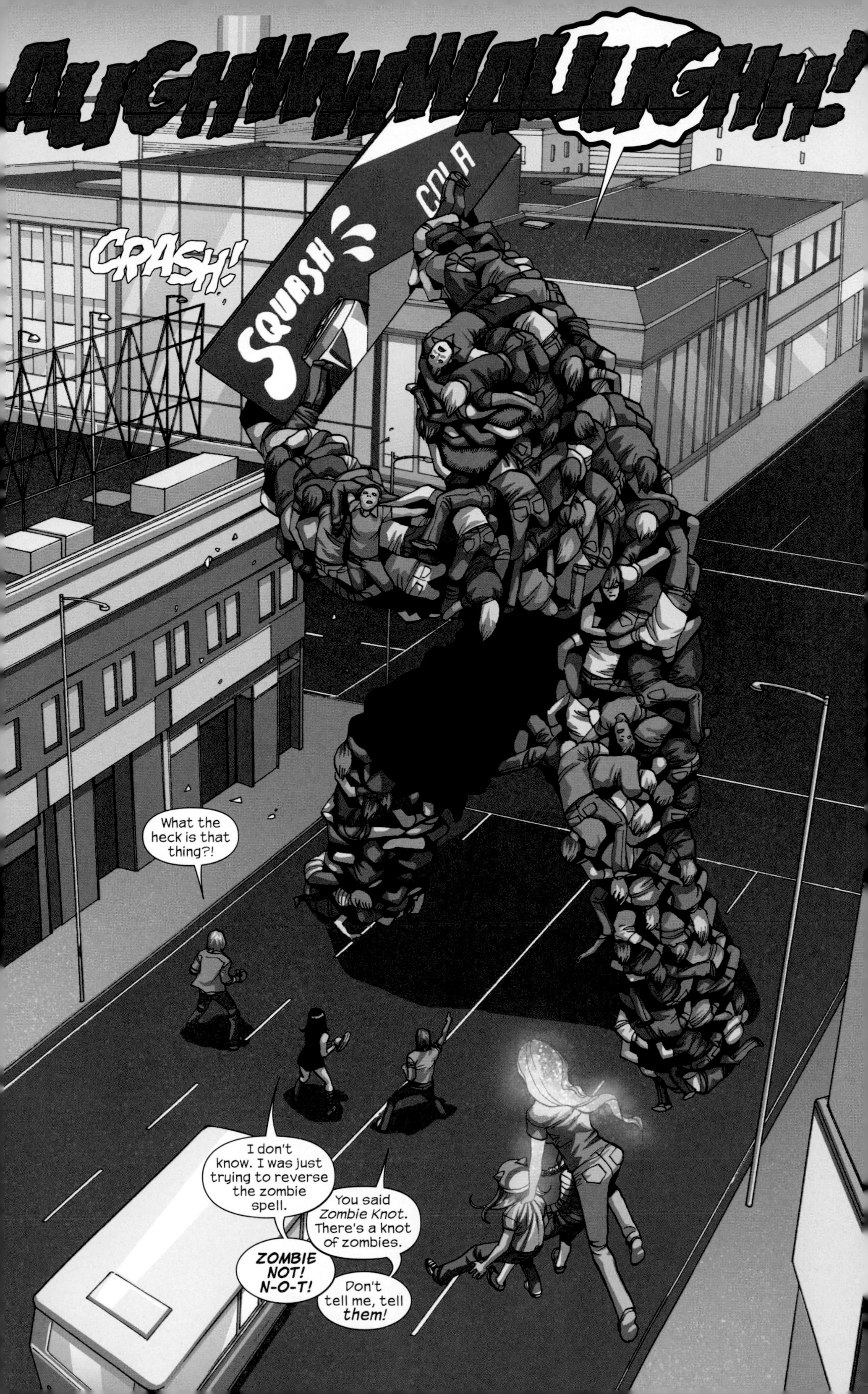
AUGHWWWAUUGHH!
CRASH!
SQUASH COLA
What the heck is that thing?!
I don't know. I was just trying to reverse the zombie spell.
You said *Zombie Knot*. There's a knot of zombies.
ZOMBIE NOT! N-O-T!
Don't tell me, tell *them!*

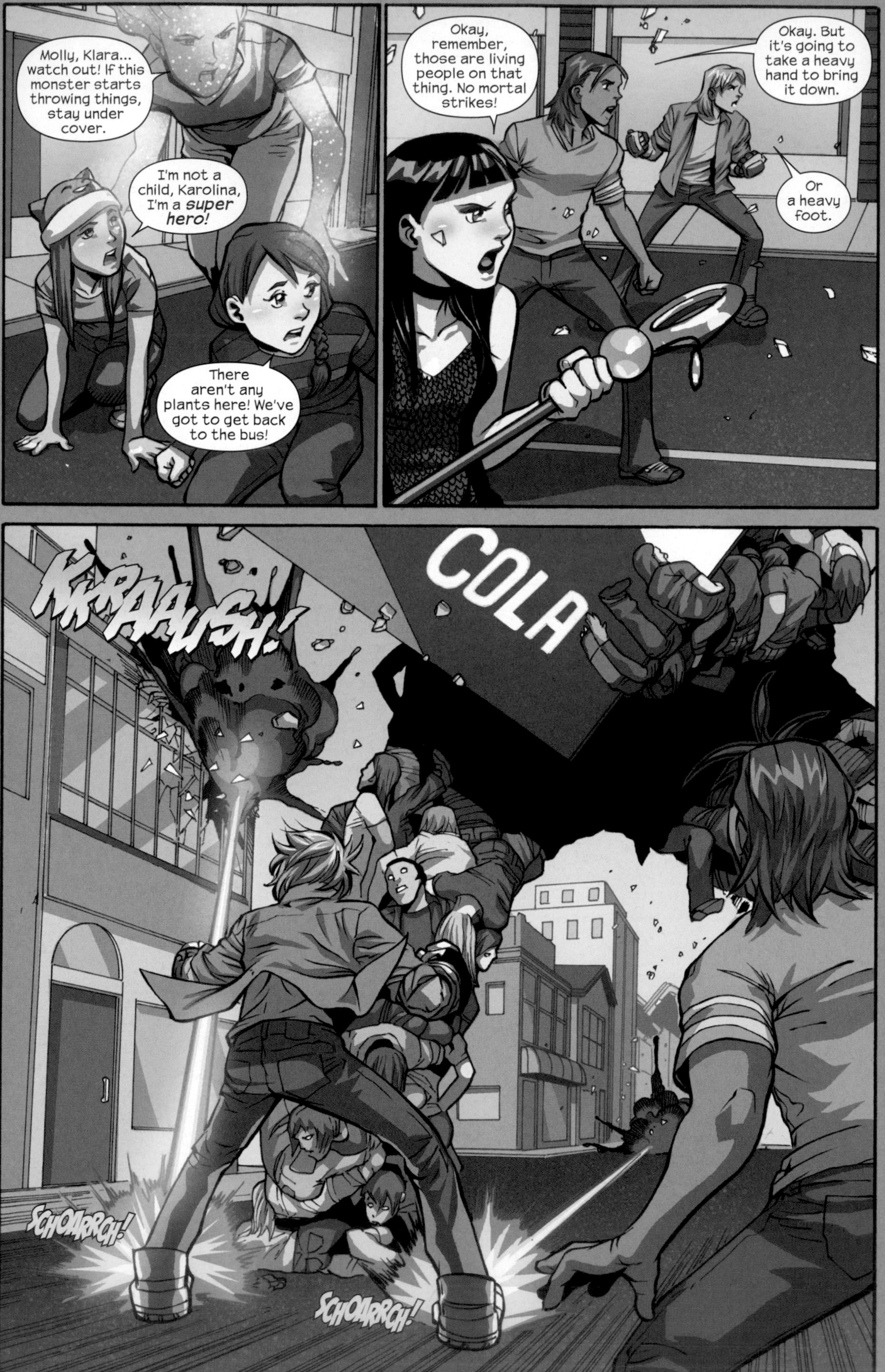
Molly, Klara... watch out! If this monster starts throwing things, stay under cover.
I'm not a child, Karolina, I'm a *super hero!*
There aren't any plants here! We've got to get back to the bus!
Okay, remember, those are living people on that thing. No mortal strikes!
Okay. But it's going to take a heavy hand to bring it down.
Or a heavy foot.
KRAAUSH!
COLA
SCHOARRCH!
SCHOARRCH!

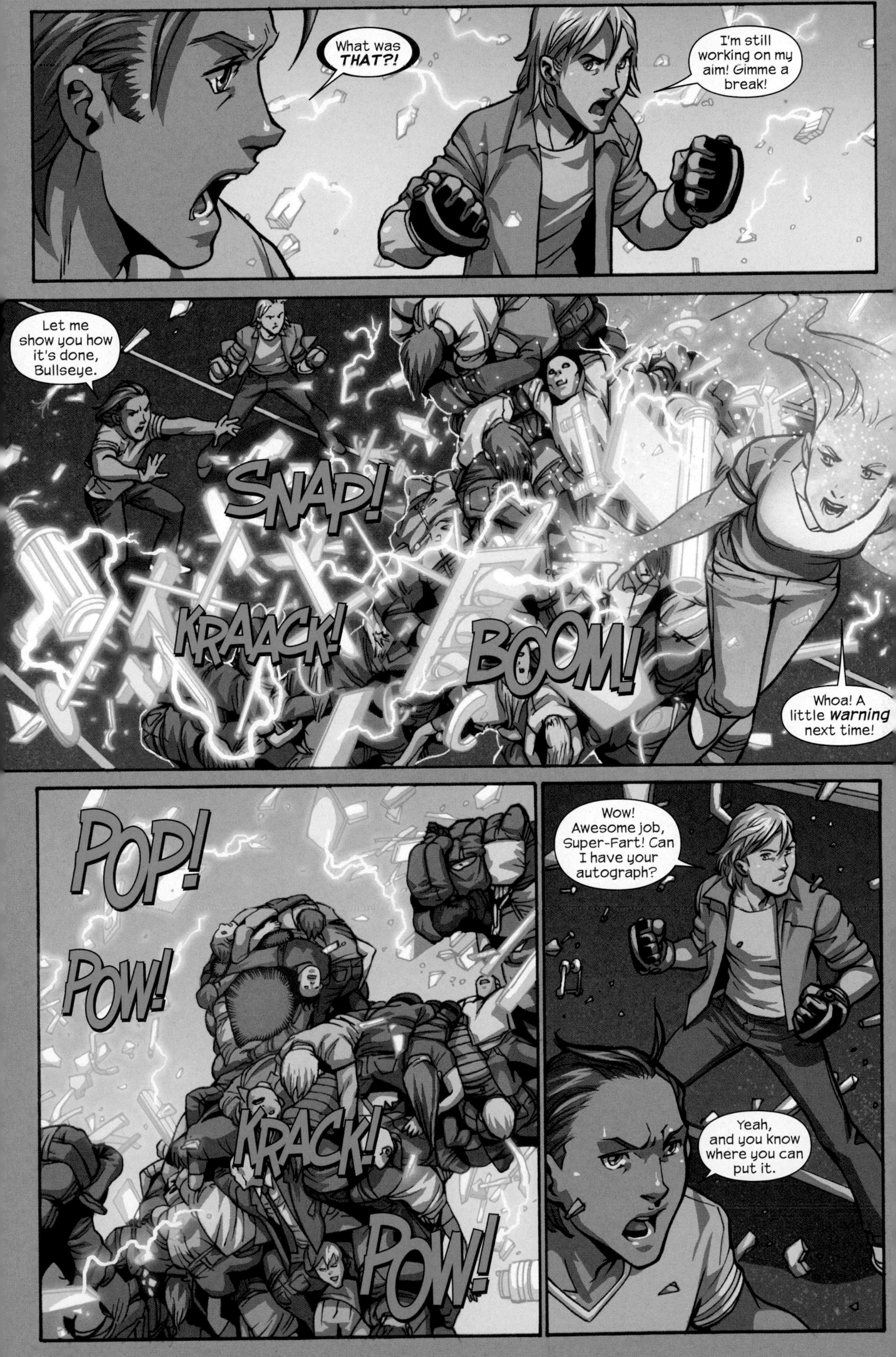

What was THAT?!
I'm still working on my aim! Gimme a break!
Let me show you how it's done, Bullseye.
SNAP!
KRAACK!
BOOM!
Whoa! A little warning next time!
POP!
POW!
KRACK!
POW!
Wow! Awesome job, Super-Fart! Can I have your autograph?
Yeah, and you know where you can put it.

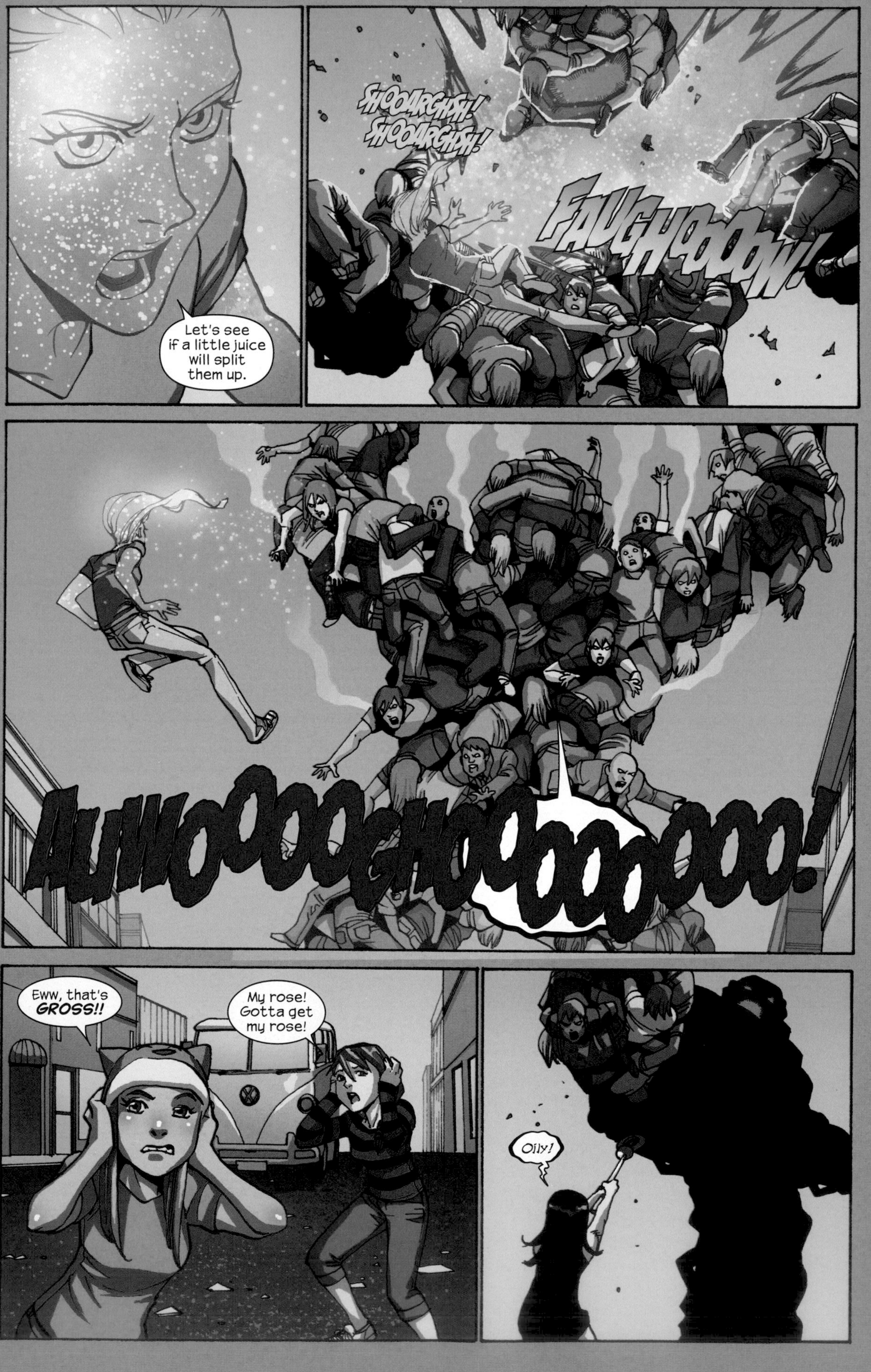
Let's see if a little juice will split them up.
SHOOARGHSH! SHOOARGHSH!
FAUGHOOOW!
AUWOOOOCHOOOOOOOO!
Eww, that's **GROSS!!**
My rose! Gotta get my rose!
Oily!

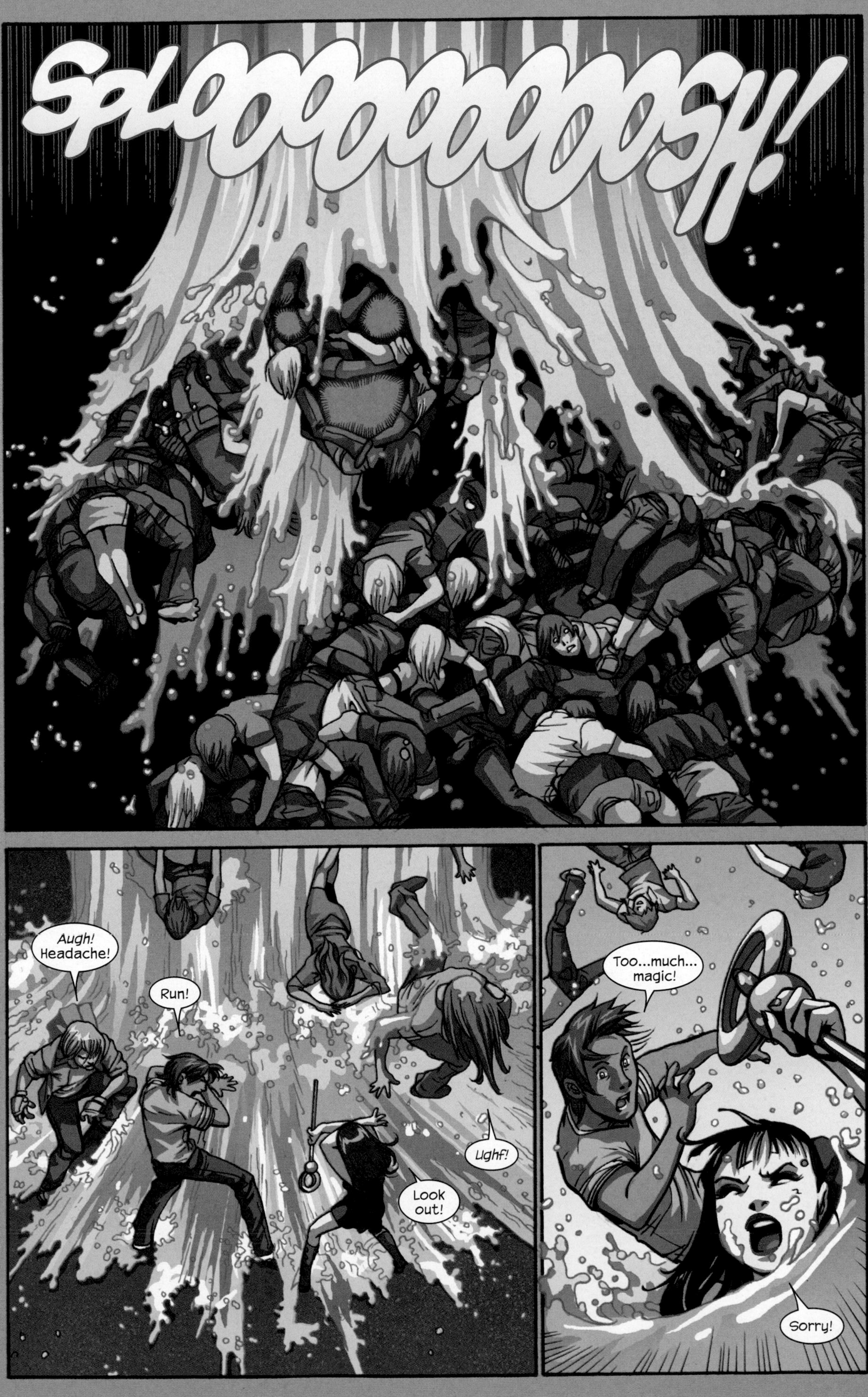
SPLOOOOOOOOSH!
Augh! Headache!
Run!
Ughf!
Look out!
Too...much... magic!
Sorry!

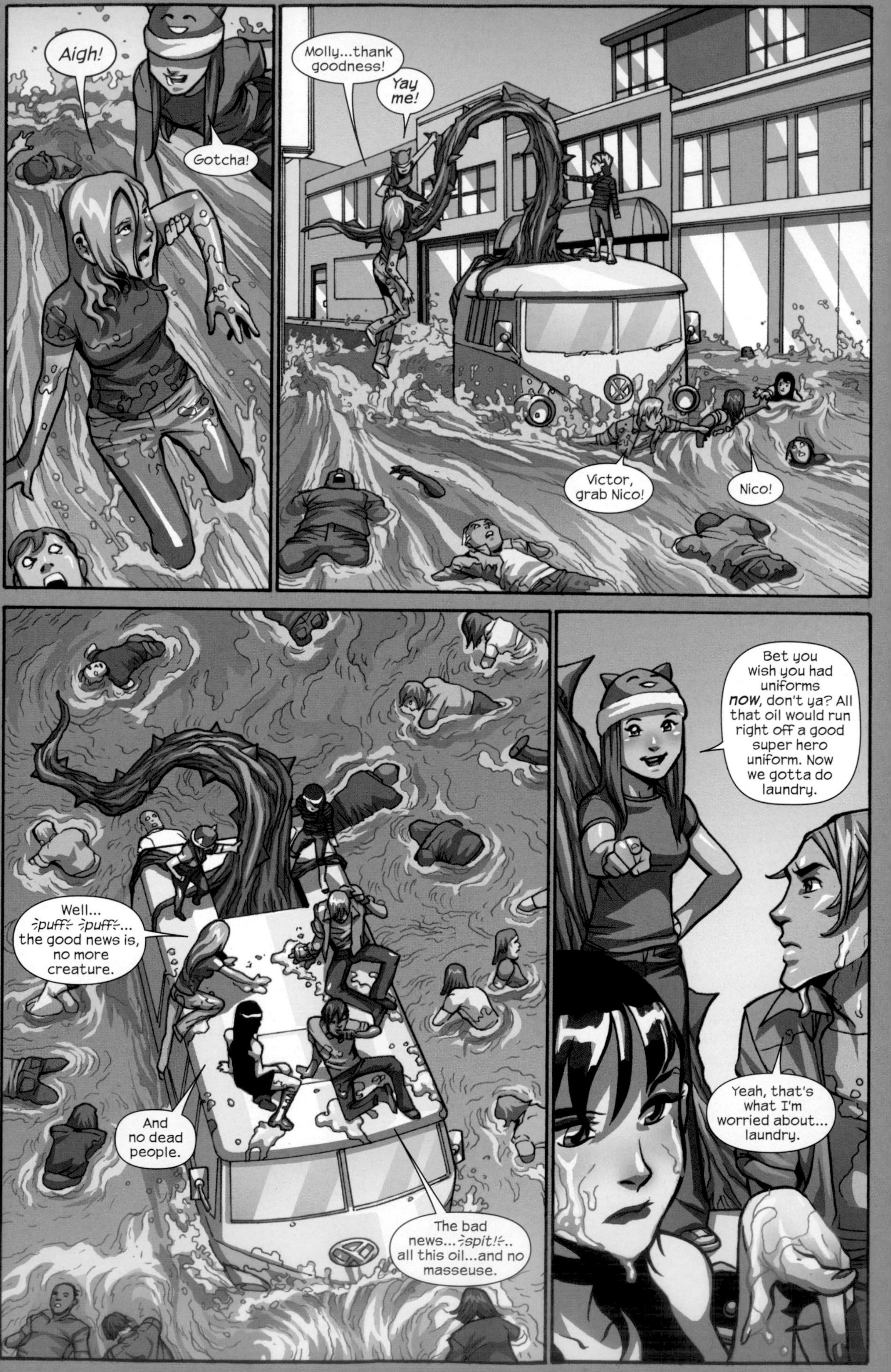
Aigh!
Gotcha!
Molly...thank goodness!
Yay me!
Victor, grab Nico!
Nico!
Well... ⁝puff⁝ ⁝puff⁝... the good news is, no more creature.
And no dead people.
The bad news... ⁝spit!⁝.. all this oil...and no masseuse.
Bet you wish you had uniforms NOW, don't ya? All that oil would run right off a good super hero uniform. Now we gotta do laundry.
Yeah, that's what I'm worried about... laundry.

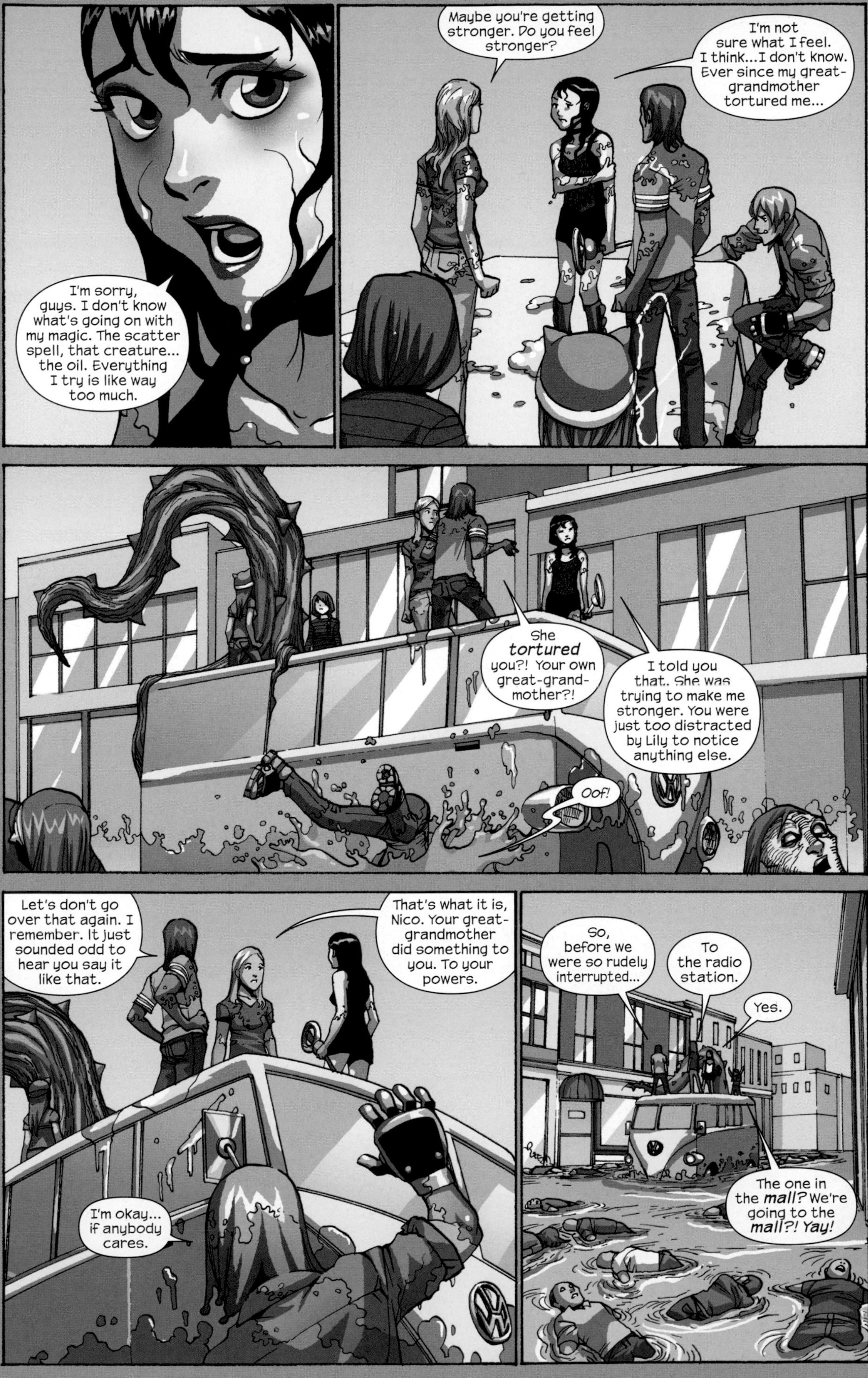
I'm sorry, guys. I don't know what's going on with my magic. The scatter spell, that creature... the oil. Everything I try is like way too much.
Maybe you're getting stronger. Do you feel stronger?
I'm not sure what I feel. I think...I don't know. Ever since my great-grandmother tortured me...
She *tortured* you?! Your own great-grand-mother?!
I told you that. She was trying to make me stronger. You were just too distracted by Lily to notice anything else.
Oof!
Let's don't go over that again. I remember. It just sounded odd to hear you say it like that.
That's what it is, Nico. Your great-grandmother did something to you. To your powers.
I'm okay... if anybody cares.
So, before we were so rudely interrupted...
To the radio station.
Yes.
The one in the *mall?* We're going to the *mall?! Yay!*

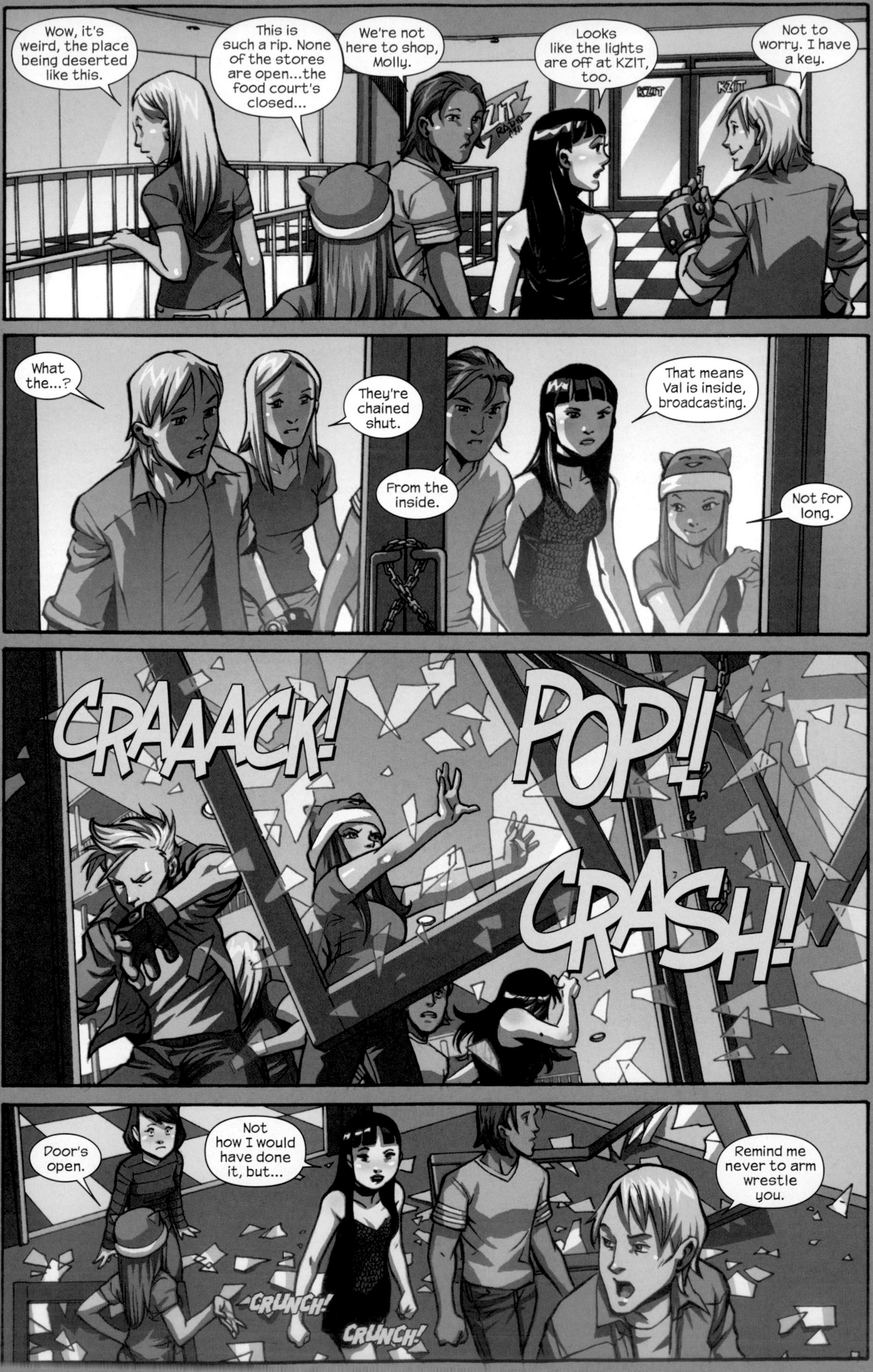

Wow, it's weird, the place being deserted like this.
This is such a rip. None of the stores are open...the food court's closed...
We're not here to shop, Molly.
Looks like the lights are off at KZIT, too.
Not to worry. I have a key.
KZIT RADIO
KZIT
KZIT
What the...?
They're chained shut.
From the inside.
That means Val is inside, broadcasting.
Not for long.
CRAAACK!
POP!!
CRASH!
Door's open.
Not how I would have done it, but...
Remind me never to arm wrestle you.
CRUNCH!
CRUNCH!

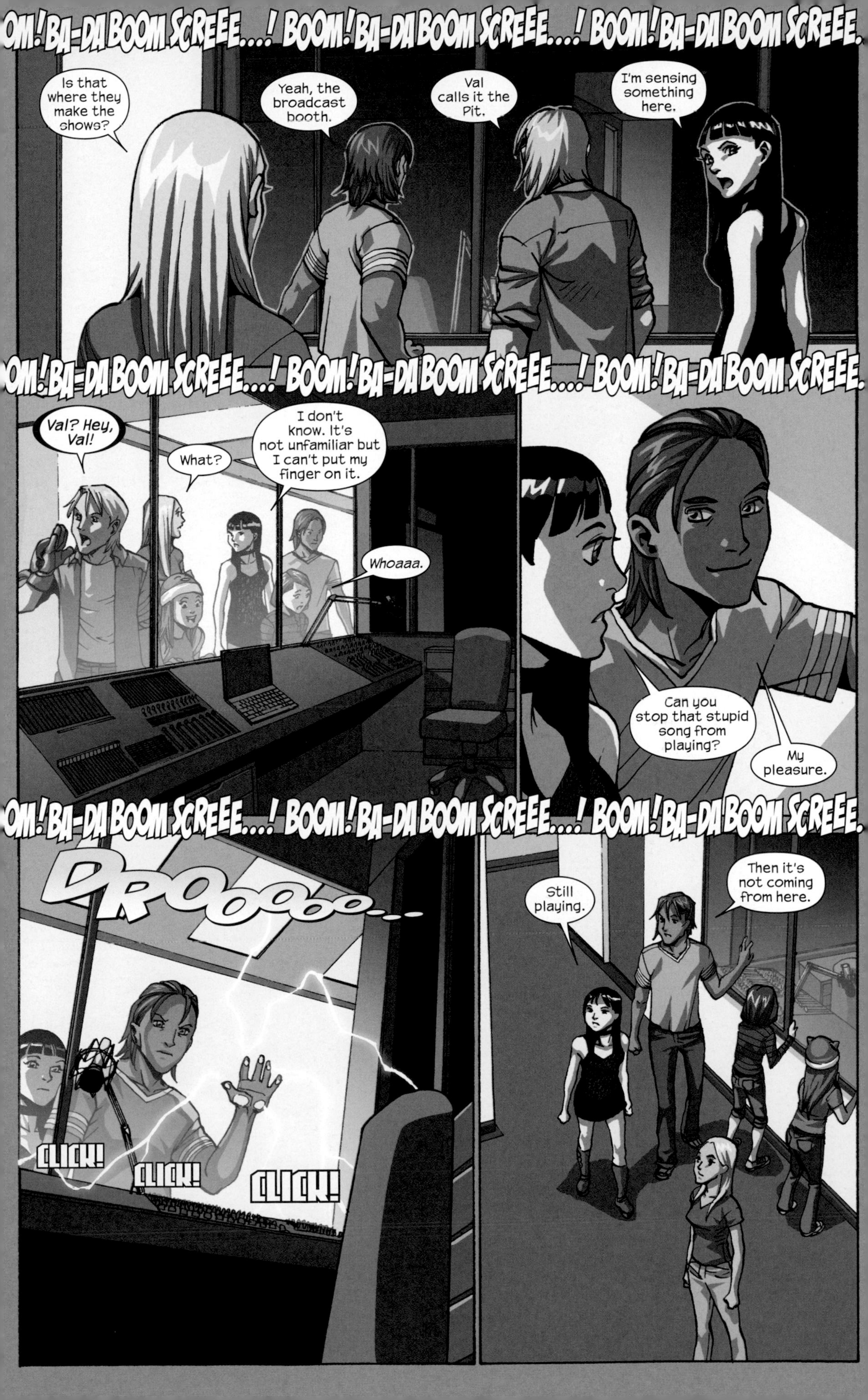
OM! BA-DA BOOM SCREEE...! BOOM! BA-DA BOOM SCREEE...! BOOM! BA-DA BOOM SCREEE.
Is that where they make the shows?
Yeah, the broadcast booth.
Val calls it the Pit.
I'm sensing something here.
OM! BA-DA BOOM SCREEE...! BOOM! BA-DA BOOM SCREEE...! BOOM! BA-DA BOOM SCREEE.
Val? Hey, Val!
What?
I don't know. It's not unfamiliar but I can't put my finger on it.
Whoaaa.
Can you stop that stupid song from playing?
My pleasure.
OM! BA-DA BOOM SCREEE...! BOOM! BA-DA BOOM SCREEE...! BOOM! BA-DA BOOM SCREEE.
DROOOOOO...
CLICK!
CLICK!
CLICK!
Still playing.
Then it's not coming from here.

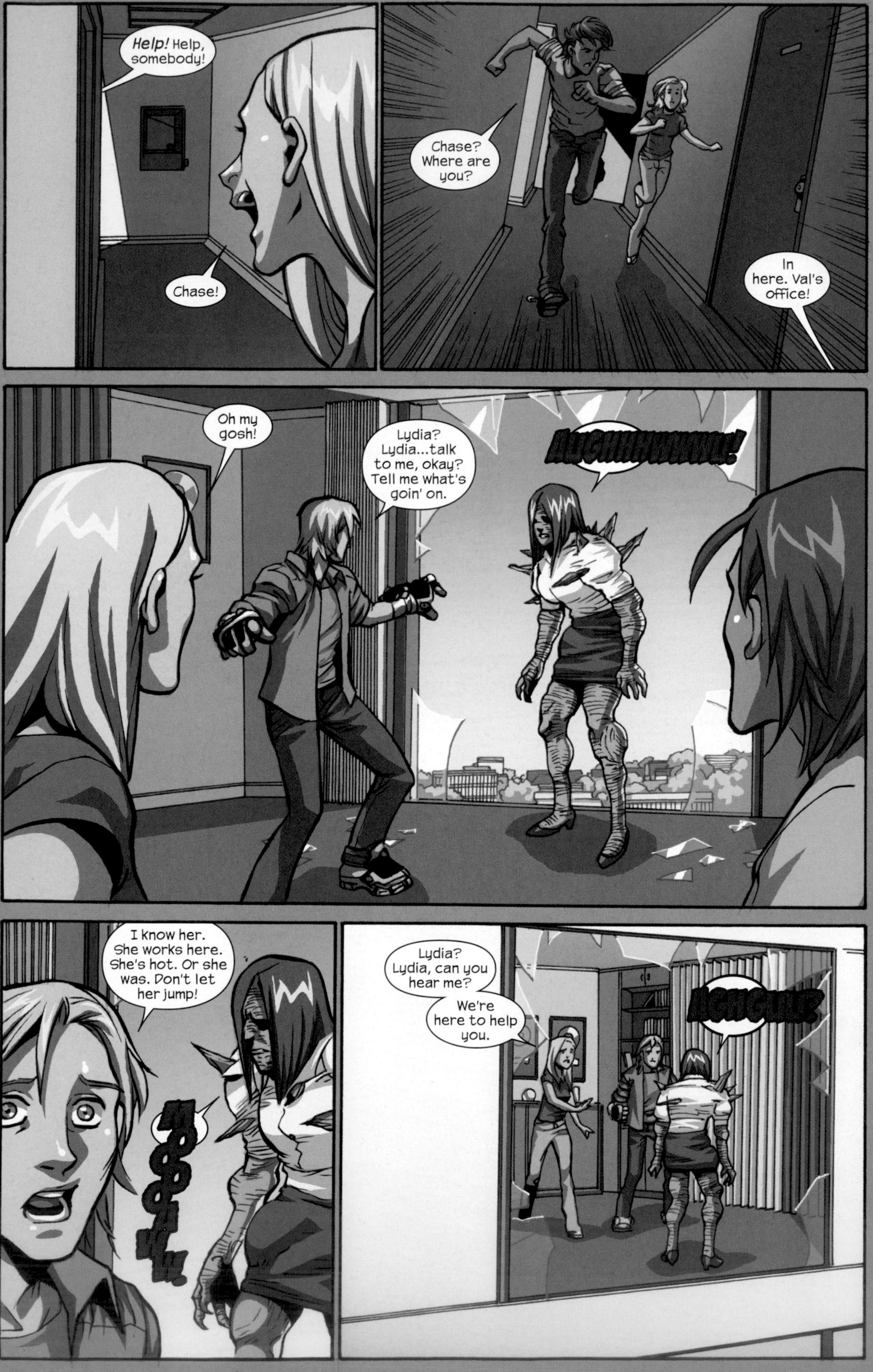
Help! Help, somebody!
Chase!
Chase? Where are you?
In here. Val's office!
Oh my gosh!
Lydia? Lydia...talk to me, okay? Tell me what's goin' on.
I know her. She works here. She's hot. Or she was. Don't let her jump!
Lydia? Lydia, can you hear me?
We're here to help you.

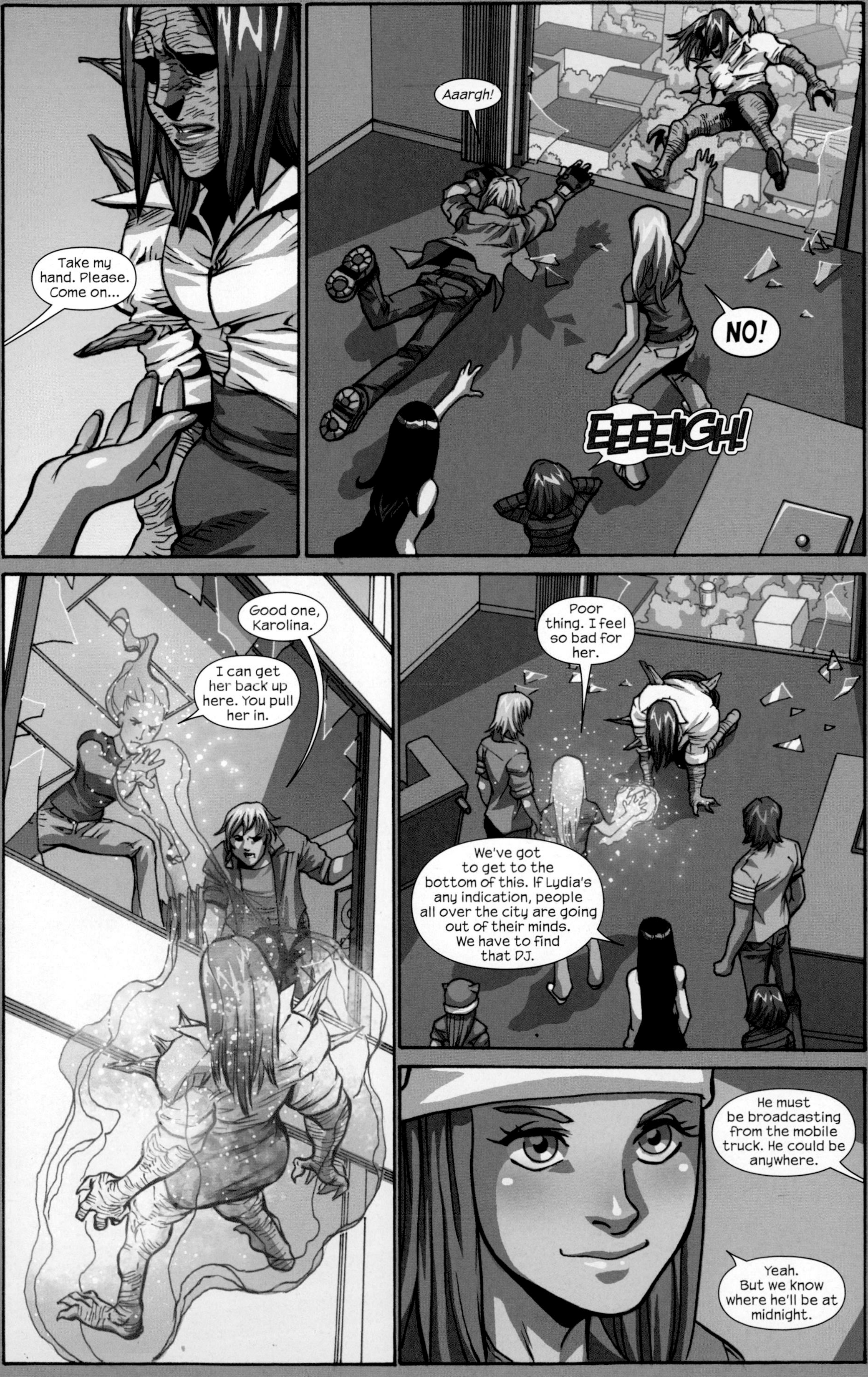
Take my hand. Please. Come on...
Aaargh!
NO!
EEEEIGH!
Good one, Karolina.
I can get her back up here. You pull her in.
Poor thing. I feel so bad for her.
We've got to get to the bottom of this. If Lydia's any indication, people all over the city are going out of their minds. We have to find that DJ.
He must be broadcasting from the mobile truck. He could be anywhere.
Yeah. But we know where he'll be at midnight.

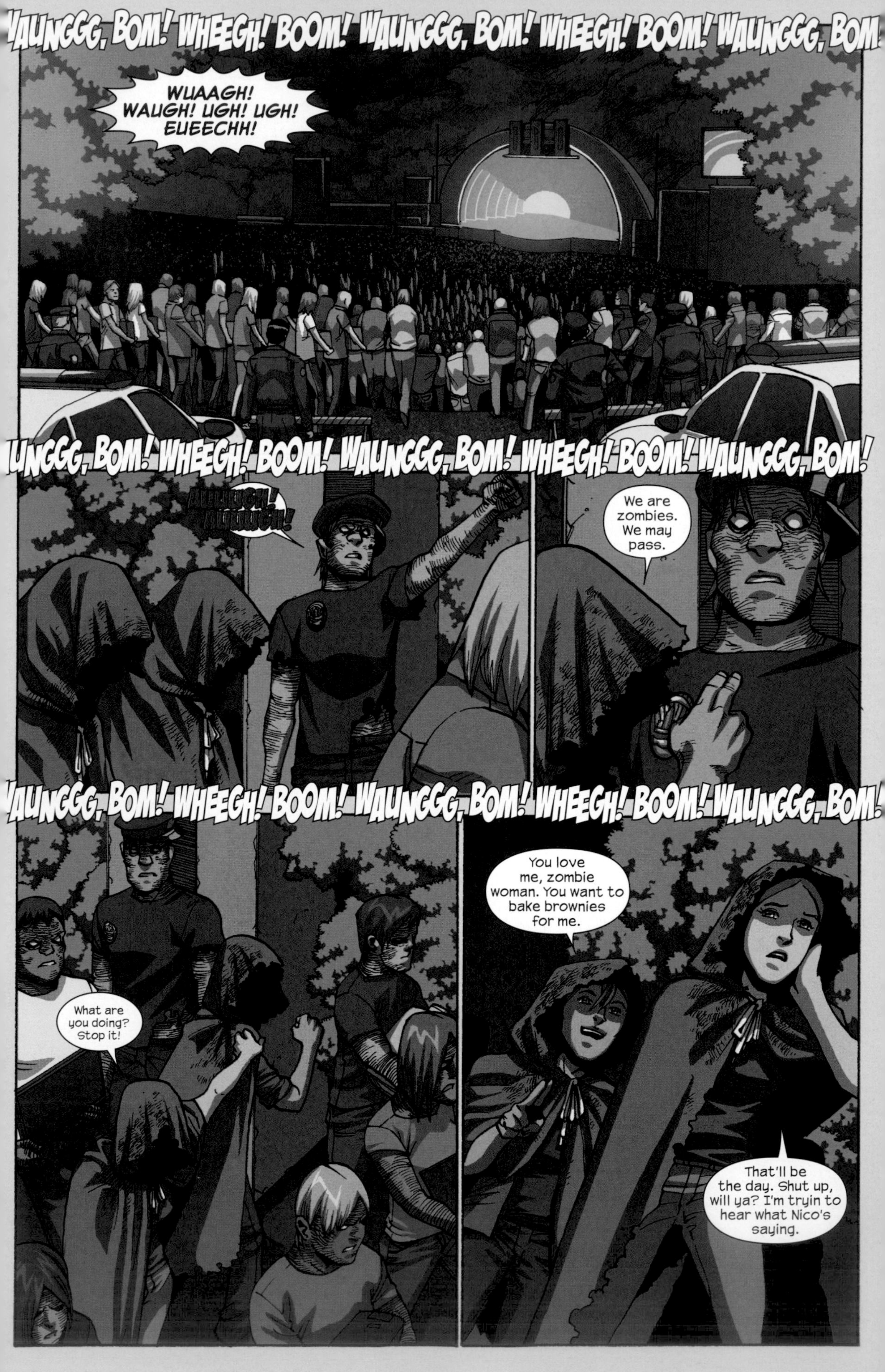

WAUNGGG, BOM! WHEEGH! BOOM! WAUNGGG, BOM! WHEEGH! BOOM! WAUNGGG, BOM!
WUAAGH! WAUGH! UGH! UGH! EUEECHH!
UNGGG, BOM! WHEEGH! BOOM! WAUNGGG, BOM! WHEEGH! BOOM! WAUNGGG, BOM!
We are zombies. We may pass.
WAUNGGG, BOM! WHEEGH! BOOM! WAUNGGG, BOM! WHEEGH! BOOM! WAUNGGG, BOM!
What are you doing? Stop it!
You love me, zombie woman. You want to bake brownies for me.
That'll be the day. Shut up, will ya? I'm tryin to hear what Nico's saying.

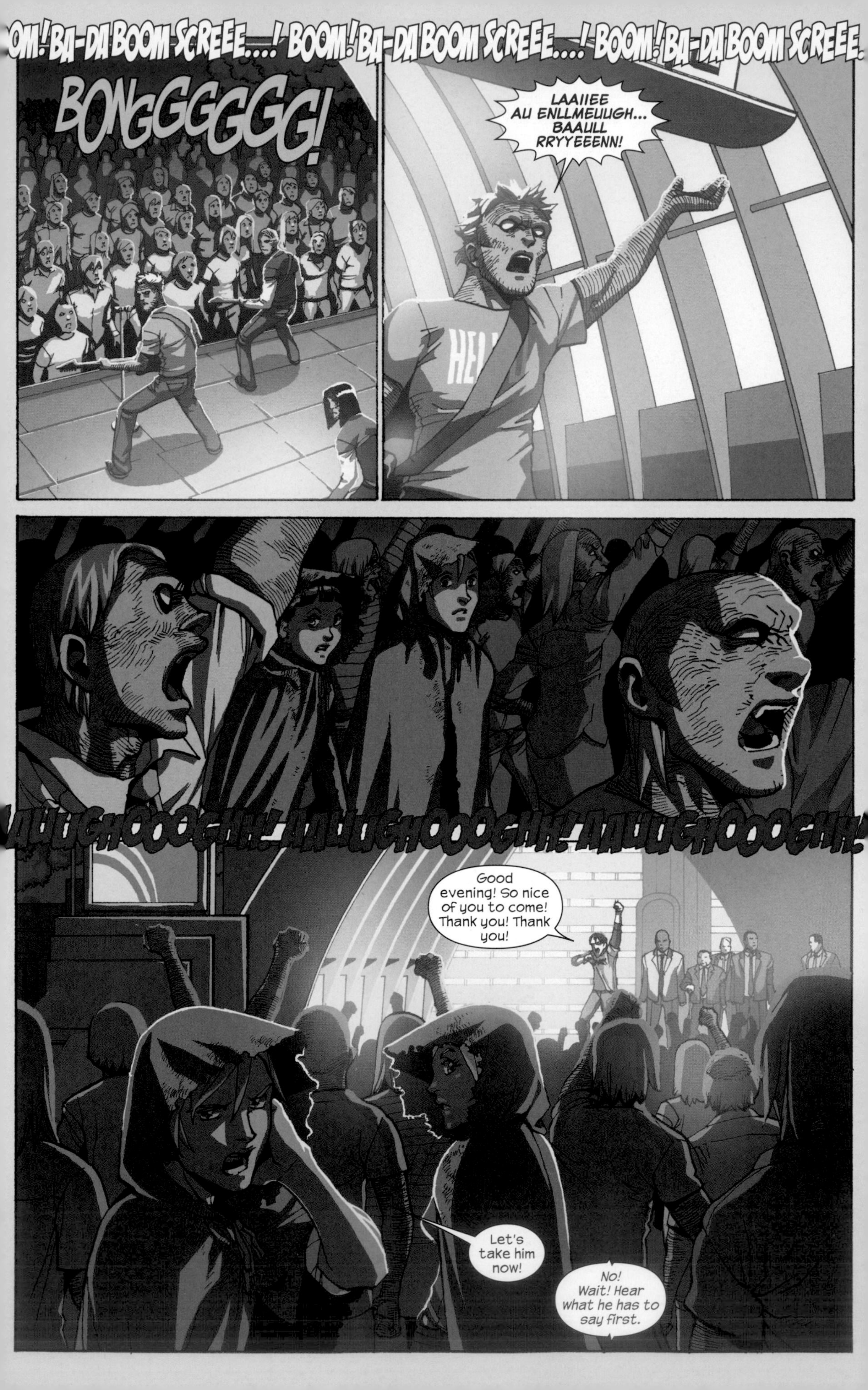
OM! BA-DA BOOM SCREEE....! BOOM! BA-DA BOOM SCREEE....! BOOM! BA-DA BOOM SCREEE.
BONGGGGGG!
LAAIIEE AU ENLLMEUUGH... BAAULL RRYYEEENN!
AAUUGHOOOOGHH! AAUUGHOOOOGHH! AAUUGHOOOOGHH!
Good evening! So nice of you to come! Thank you! Thank you!
Let's take him now!
No! Wait! Hear what he has to say first.

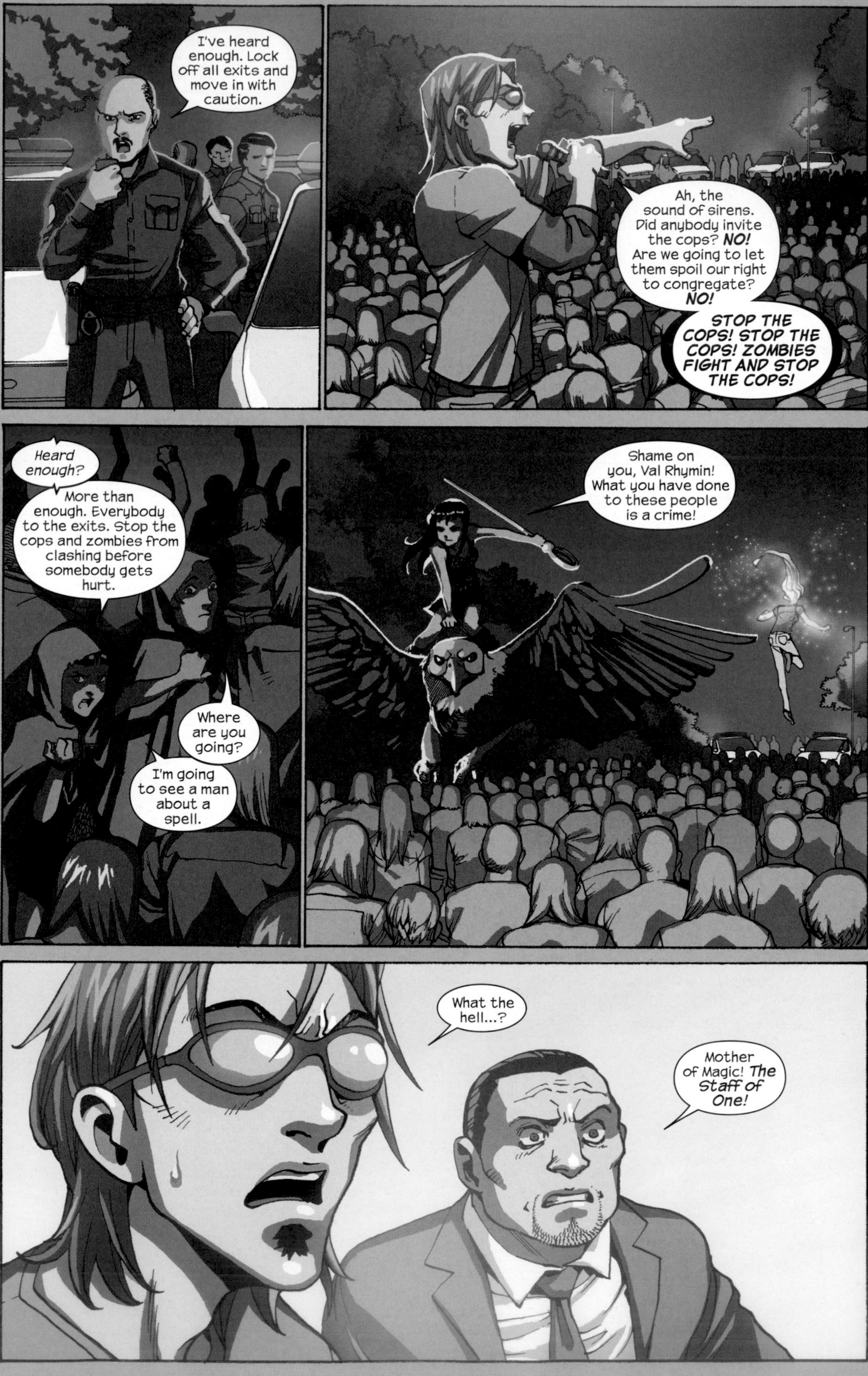
I've heard enough. Lock off all exits and move in with caution.
Ah, the sound of sirens. Did anybody invite the cops? NO! Are we going to let them spoil our right to congregate? NO!
STOP THE COPS! STOP THE COPS! ZOMBIES FIGHT AND STOP THE COPS!
Heard enough?
More than enough. Everybody to the exits. Stop the cops and zombies from clashing before somebody gets hurt.
Where are you going?
I'm going to see a man about a spell.
Shame on you, Val Rhymin! What you have done to these people is a crime!
What the hell...?
Mother of Magic! The Staff of One!

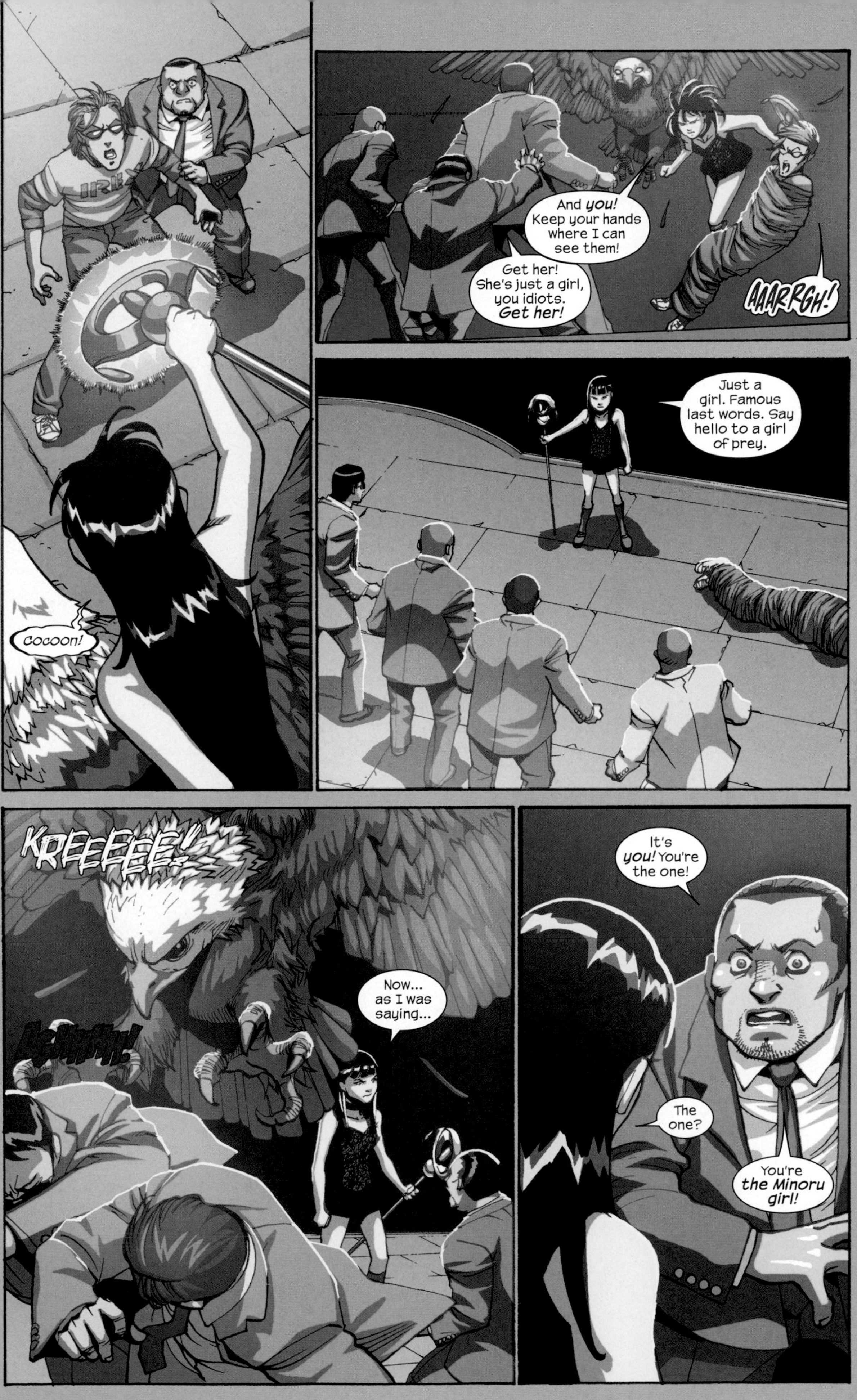

Cocoon!
And *you!* Keep your hands where I can see them!
Get her! She's just a girl, you idiots. *Get her!*
AAARRGH!
Just a girl. Famous last words. Say hello to a girl of prey.
KREEEEEE!
Now... as I was saying...
It's *you!* You're the one!
The one?
You're *the Minoru girl!*

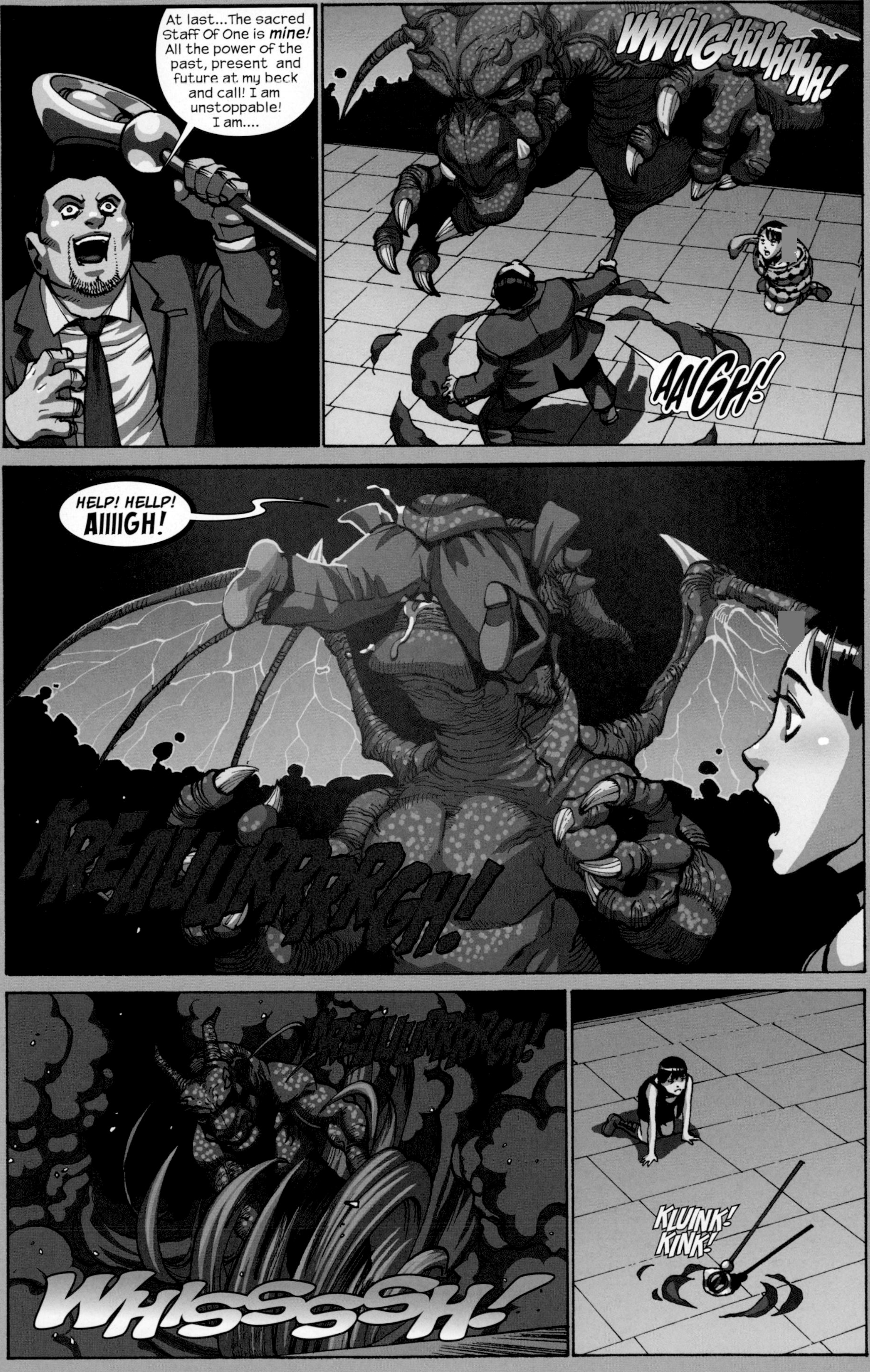
At last...The sacred Staff Of One is *mine!* All the power of the past, present and future at my beck and call! I am unstoppable! I am....
WWIIIGHHHHHH!
AAIGH!
HELP! HELLP! AIIIIGH!
KREEUURRRGH!
WHISSSSH!
KLUINK! KINK!

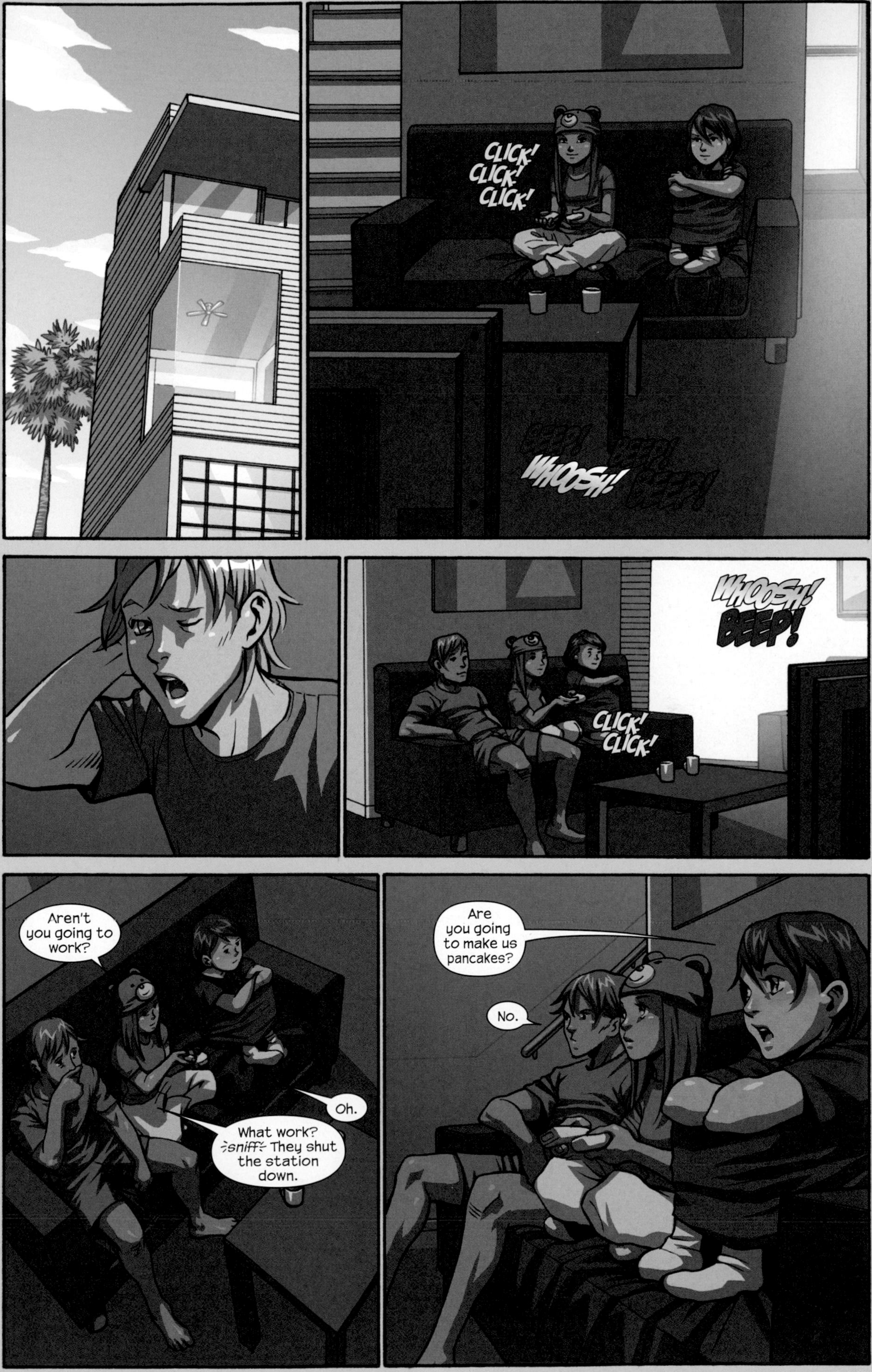
CLICK! CLICK! CLICK!
WHOOSH!
WHOOSH! BEEP!
CLICK! CLICK!
Aren't you going to work?
What work? -sniff- They shut the station down.
Oh.
Are you going to make us pancakes?
No.

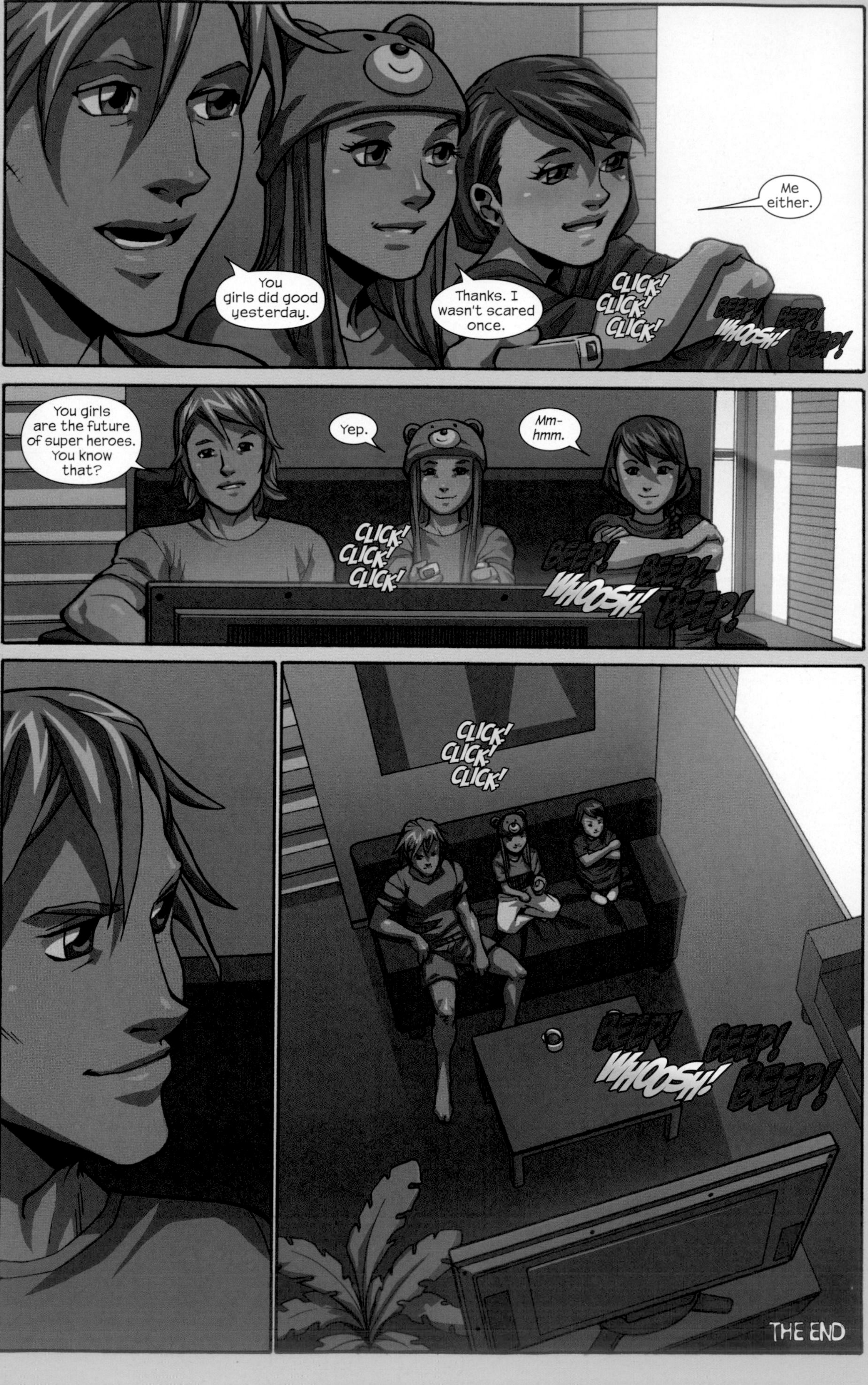

You girls did good yesterday.
Thanks. I wasn't scared once.
Me either.
CLICK! CLICK! CLICK!
BEEP! WHOOSH! BEEP! BEEP!
You girls are the future of super heroes. You know that?
Yep.
Mm-hmm.
CLICK! CLICK! CLICK!
BEEP! WHOOSH! BEEP! BEEP!
CLICK! CLICK! CLICK!
BEEP! WHOOSH! BEEP! BEEP!
THE END

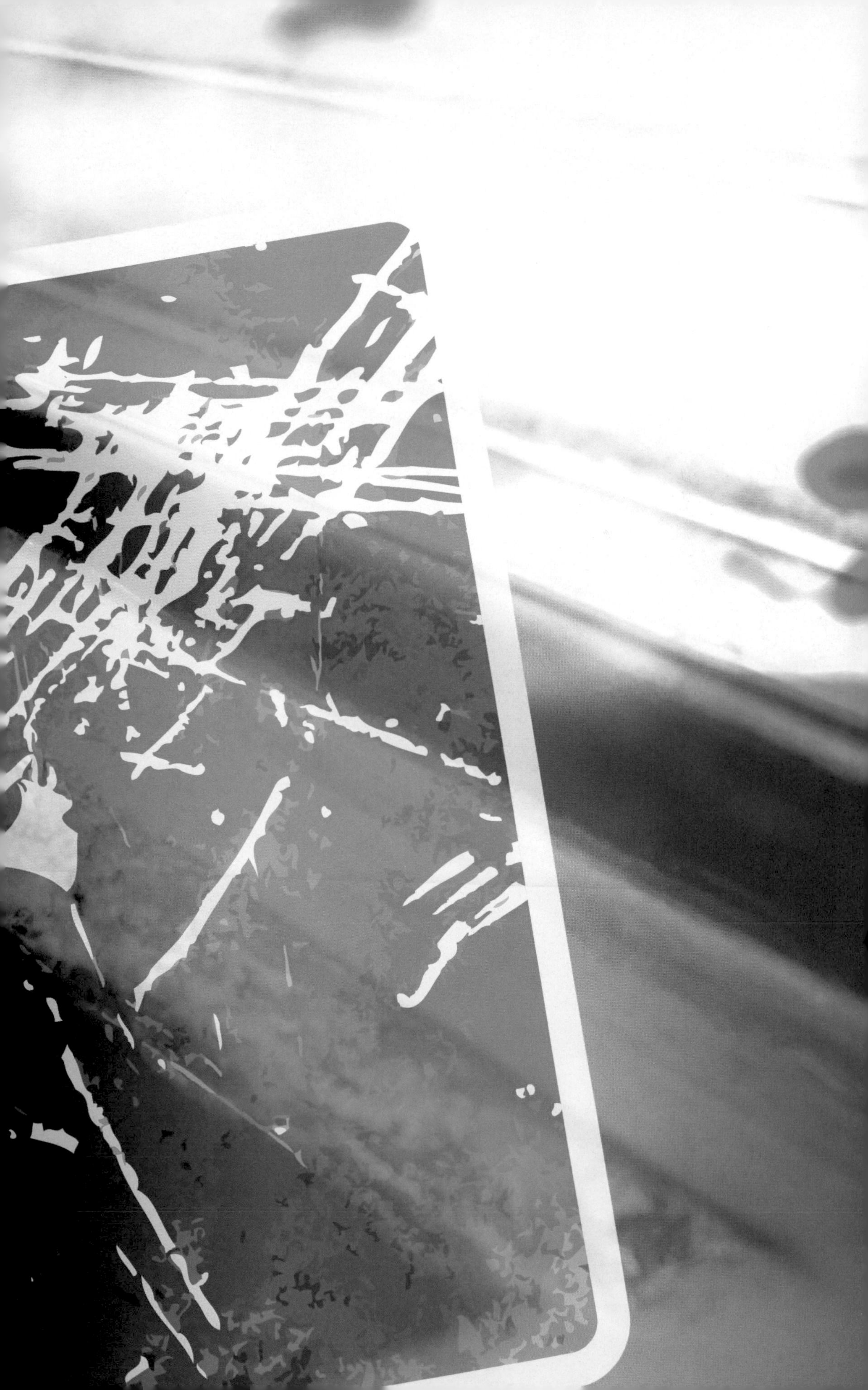

10

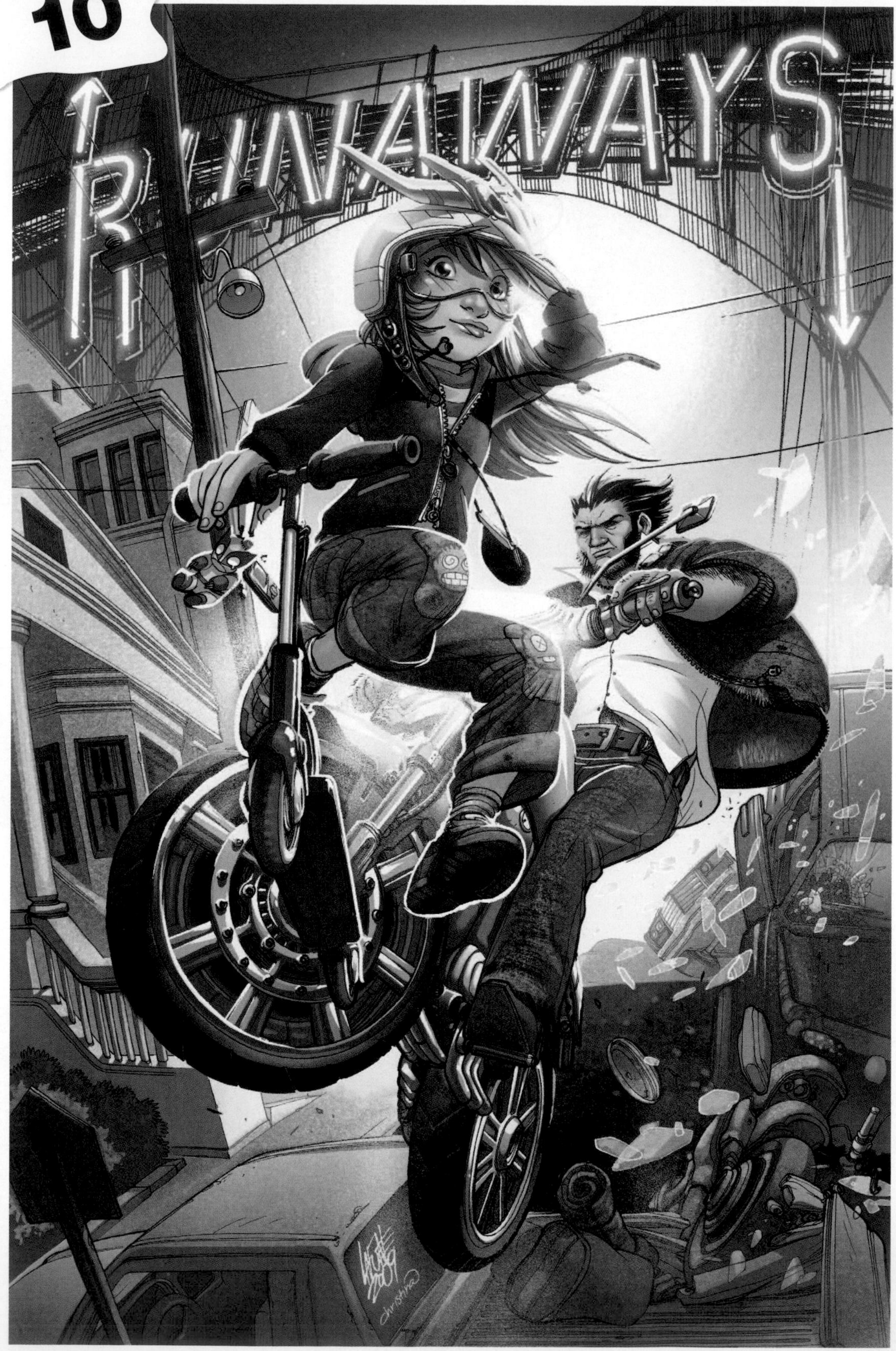

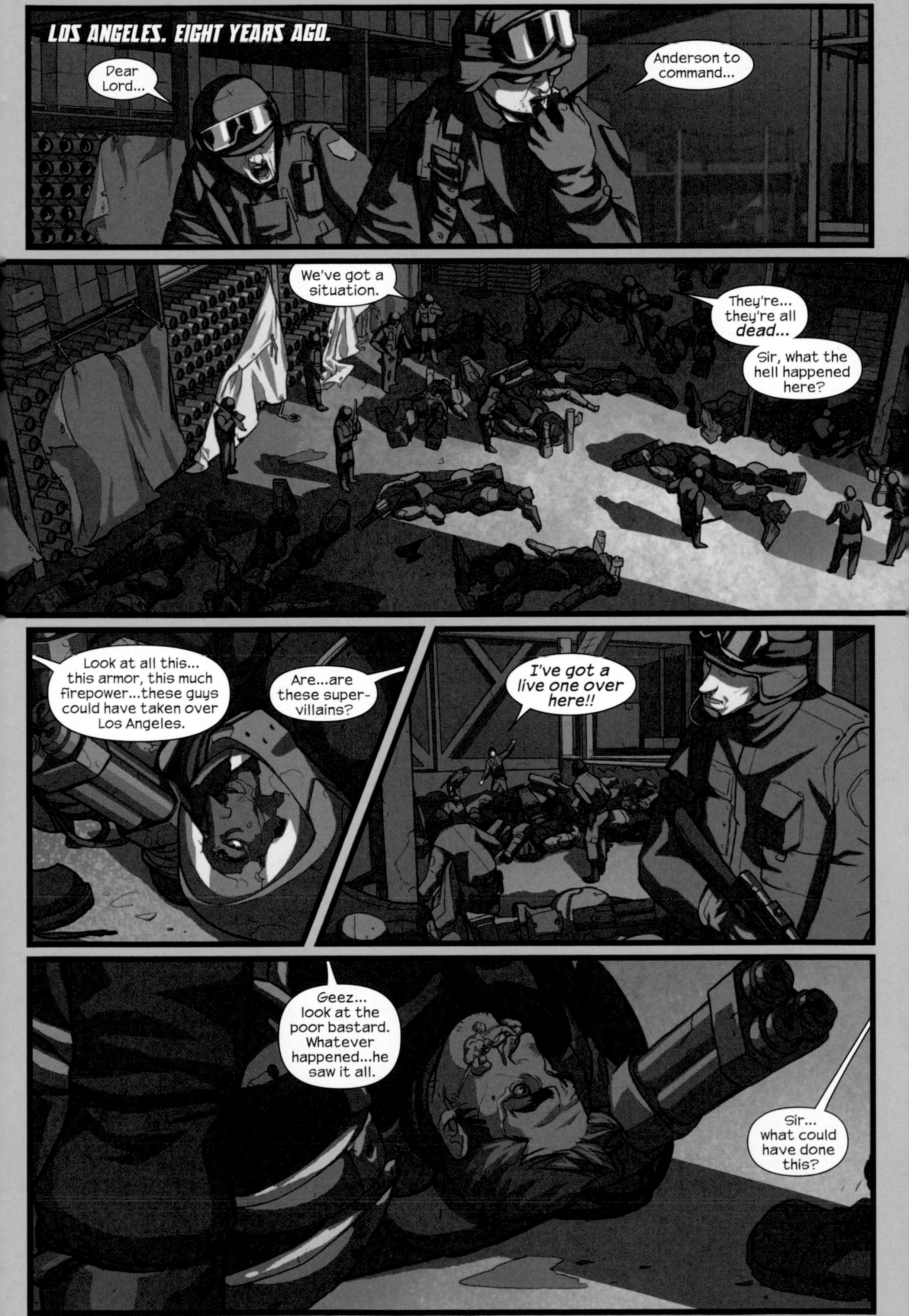
LOS ANGELES. EIGHT YEARS AGO.
Dear Lord...
Anderson to command...
We've got a situation.
They're... they're all *dead...*
Sir, what the hell happened here?
Look at all this... this armor, this much firepower...these guys could have taken over Los Angeles.
Are...are these super-villains?
I've got a live one over here!!
Geez... look at the poor bastard. Whatever happened...he saw it all.
Sir... what could have done this?

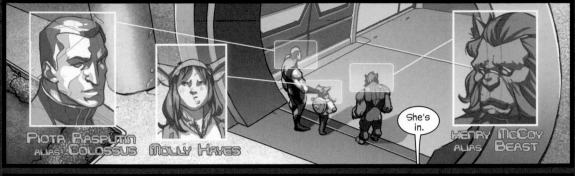

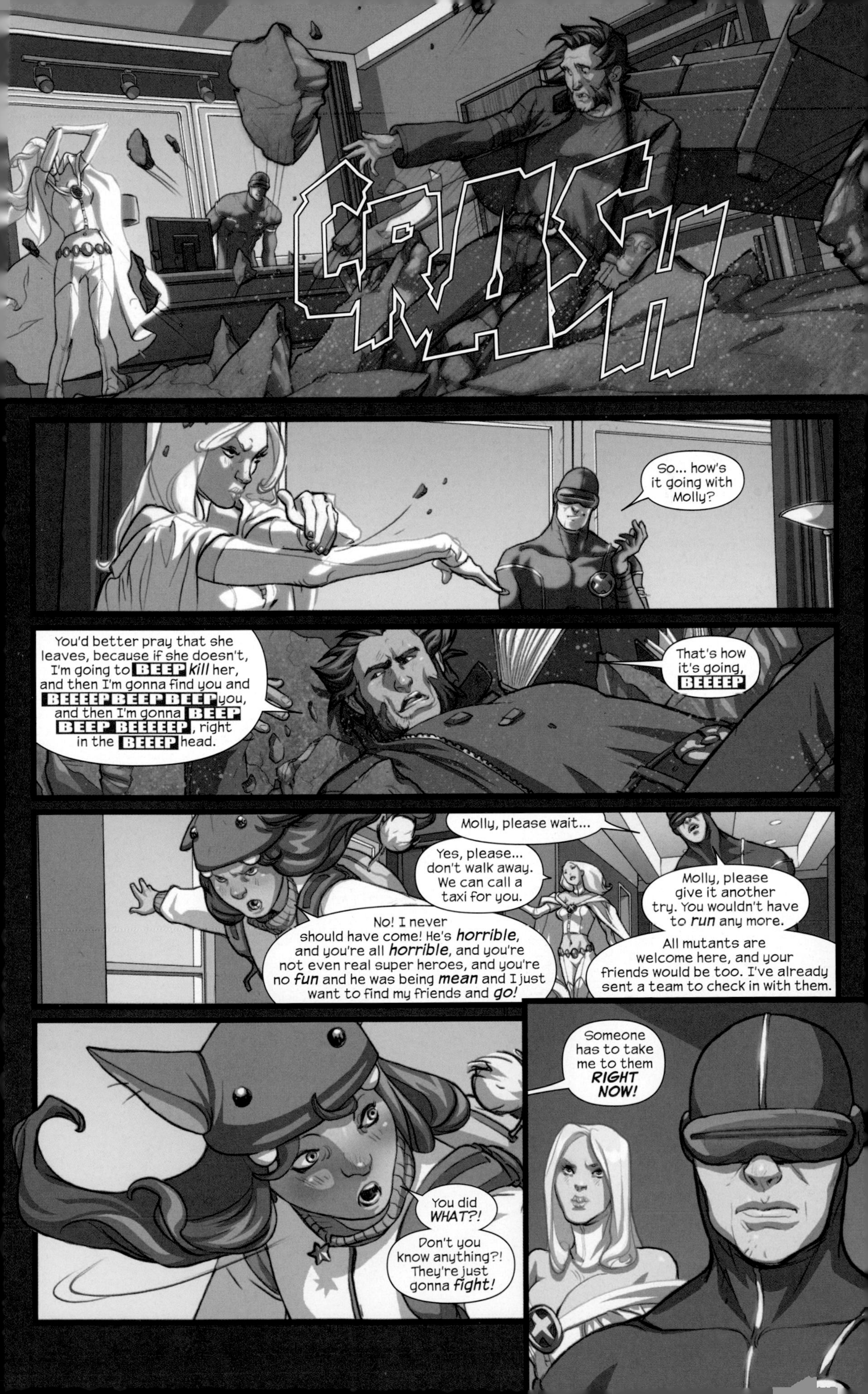
CRASH
So... how's it going with Molly?
You'd better pray that she leaves, because if she doesn't, I'm going to BEEP *kill* her, and then I'm gonna find you and BEEEEP BEEP BEEP you, and then I'm gonna BEEP BEEP BEEEEEP, right in the BEEEP head.
That's how it's going, BEEEEP
Molly, please wait...
Yes, please... don't walk away. We can call a taxi for you.
Molly, please give it another try. You wouldn't have to *run* any more.
No! I never should have come! He's *horrible*, and you're all *horrible*, and you're not even real super heroes, and you're no *fun* and he was being *mean* and I just want to find my friends and *go!*
All mutants are welcome here, and your friends would be too. I've already sent a team to check in with them.
You did *WHAT?!*
Don't you know anything?! They're just gonna *fight!*
Someone has to take me to them *RIGHT NOW!*

So we have to make a stop... I'm gonna go get this special *sword*, and I need you to cut off my *head* with it.

No. And that's *gross*.

Your parents were all super-villains, is that it? You gotta be kidding me.

I mean, what the hell kind of super-villains raised *you*? Evil Care Bears? My Little Evil Pony?

Don't you talk about my mom and dad!

You woulda been better off if they made *you* evil, too. At least then you'd have a better picture of how the world actually works, 'cuz right now--

SNFF!

Are...are you smelling me?

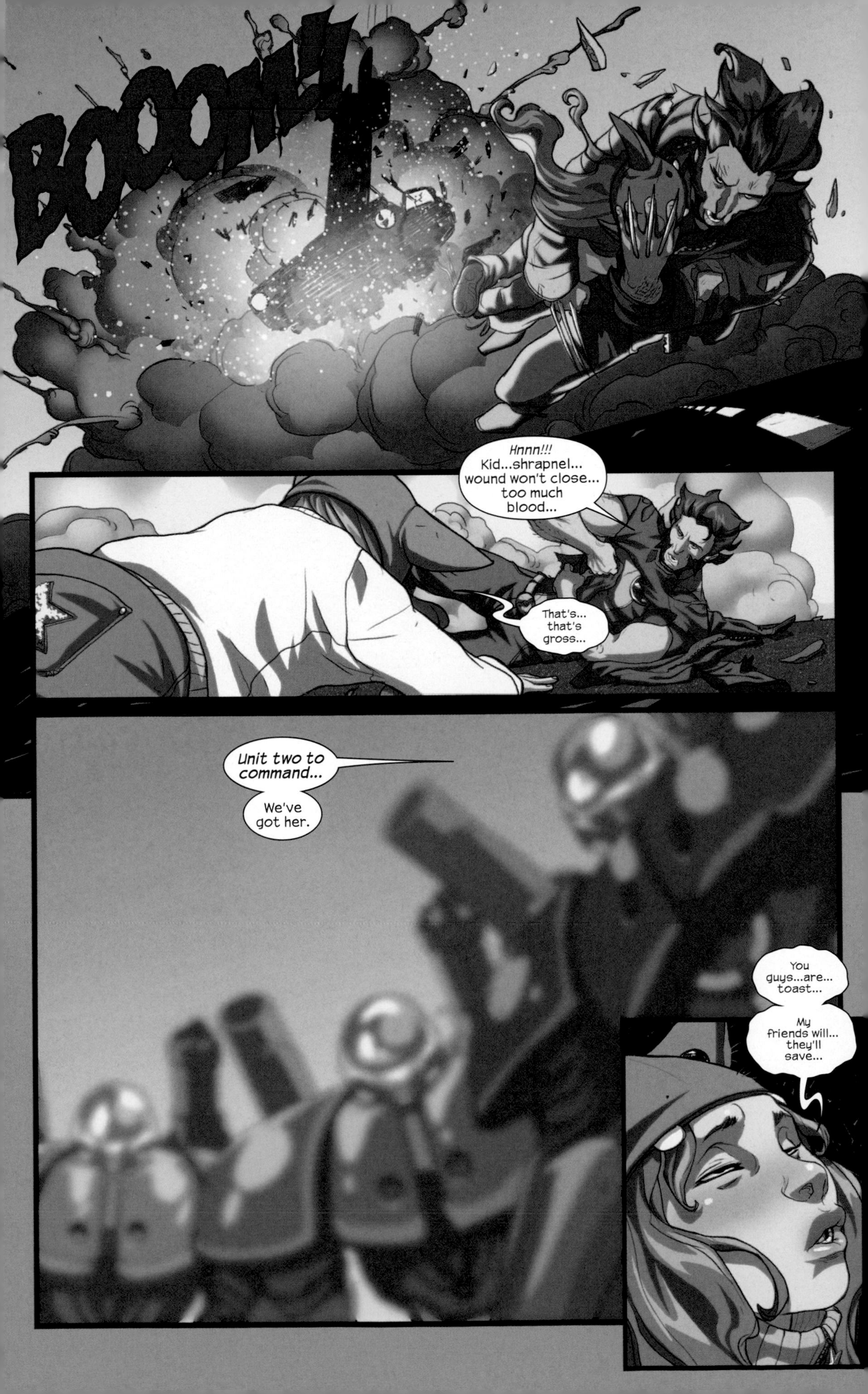
BOOOM!!
Hnnn!!! Kid...shrapnel... wound won't close... too much blood...
That's... that's gross...
Unit two to command...
We've got her.
You guys...are... toast...
My friends will... they'll save...

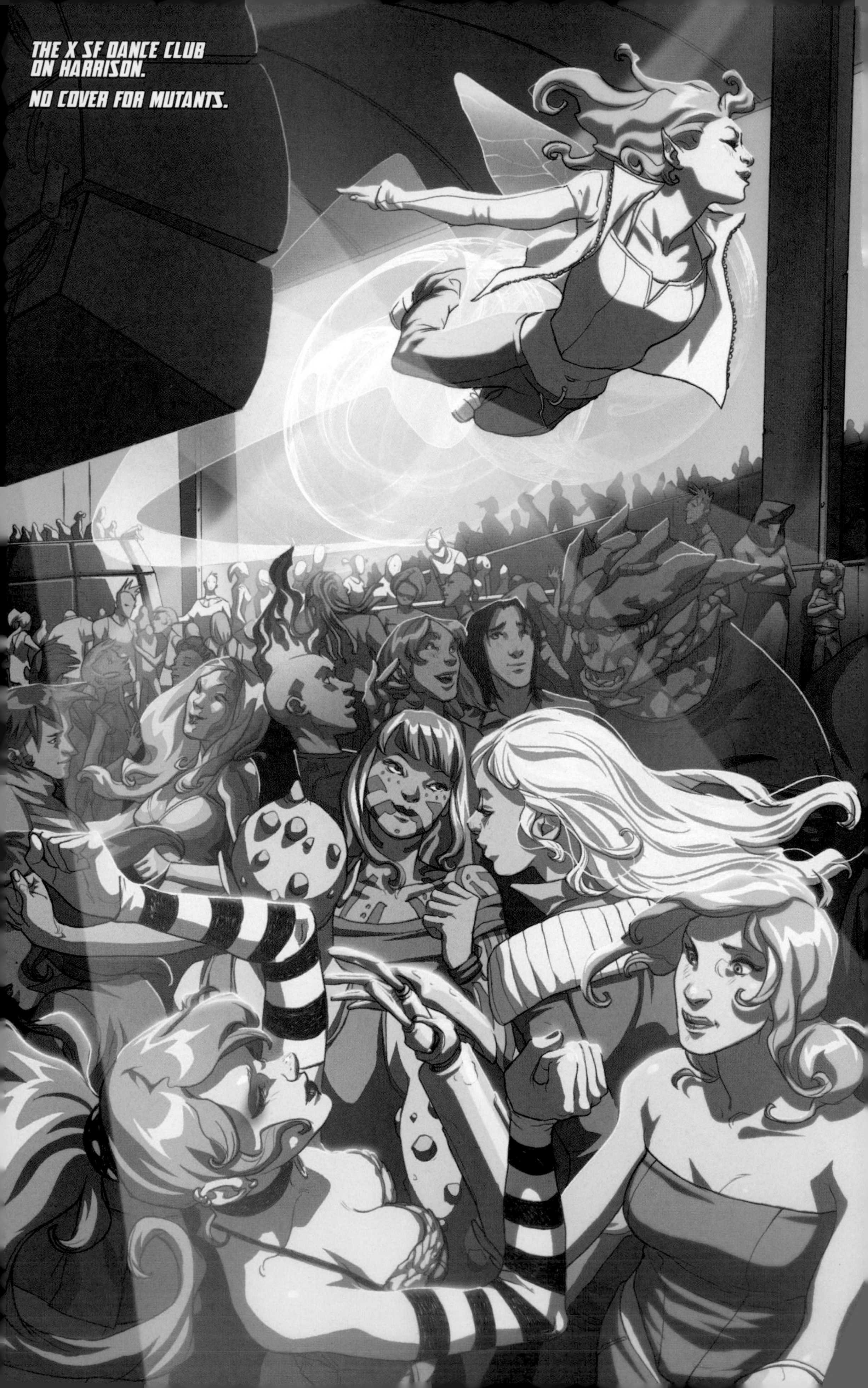
THE X SF DANCE CLUB ON HARRISON.
NO COVER FOR MUTANTS.

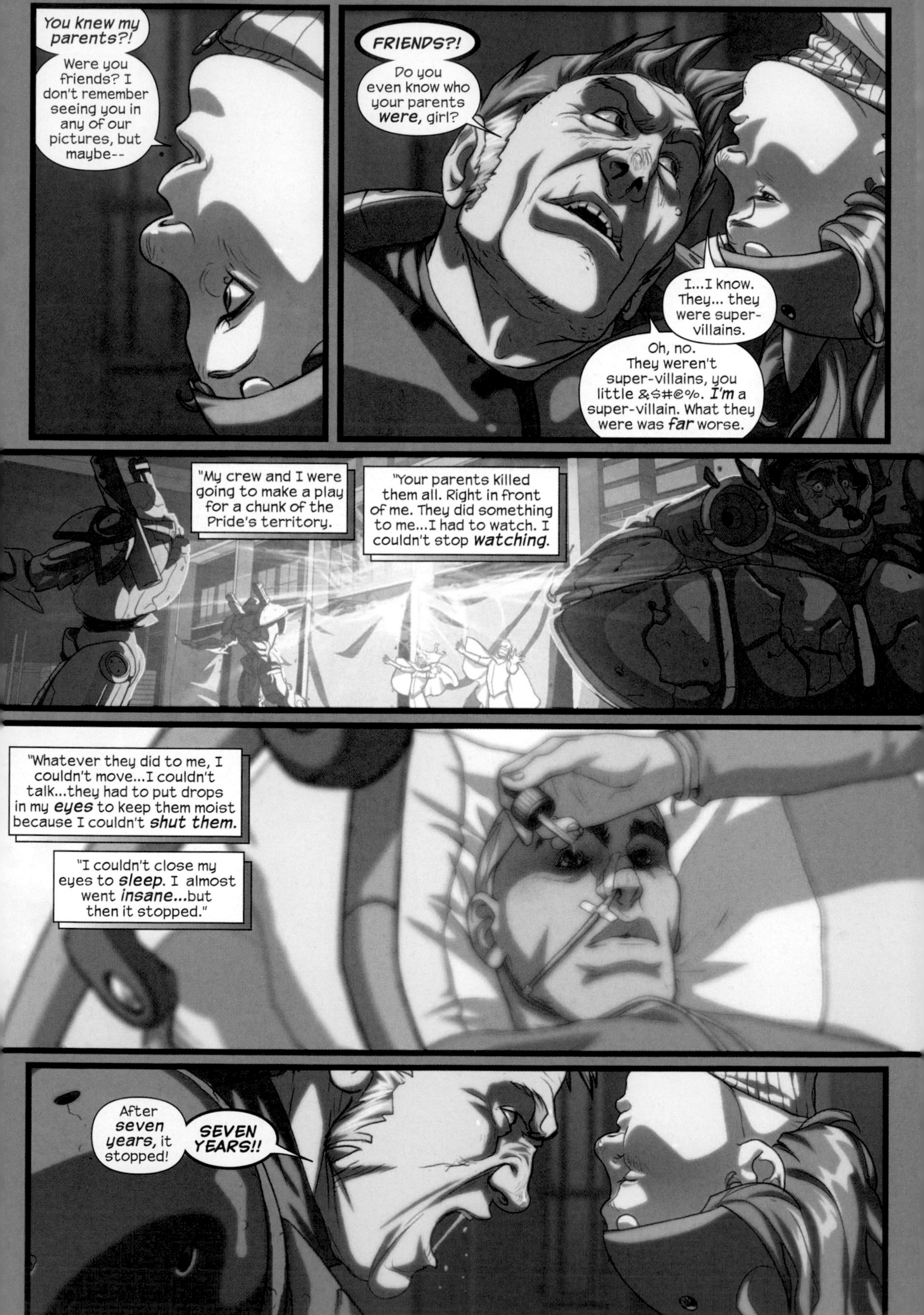
You knew my parents?!
Were you friends? I don't remember seeing you in any of our pictures, but maybe--
FRIENDS?!
Do you even know who your parents were, girl?
I...I know. They... they were super-villains.
Oh, no. They weren't super-villains, you little &$#@%. I'm a super-villain. What they were was far worse.
"My crew and I were going to make a play for a chunk of the Pride's territory.
"Your parents killed them all. Right in front of me. They did something to me...I had to watch. I couldn't stop watching.
"Whatever they did to me, I couldn't move...I couldn't talk...they had to put drops in my eyes to keep them moist because I couldn't shut them.
"I couldn't close my eyes to sleep. I almost went insane...but then it stopped."
After seven years, it stopped!
SEVEN YEARS!!

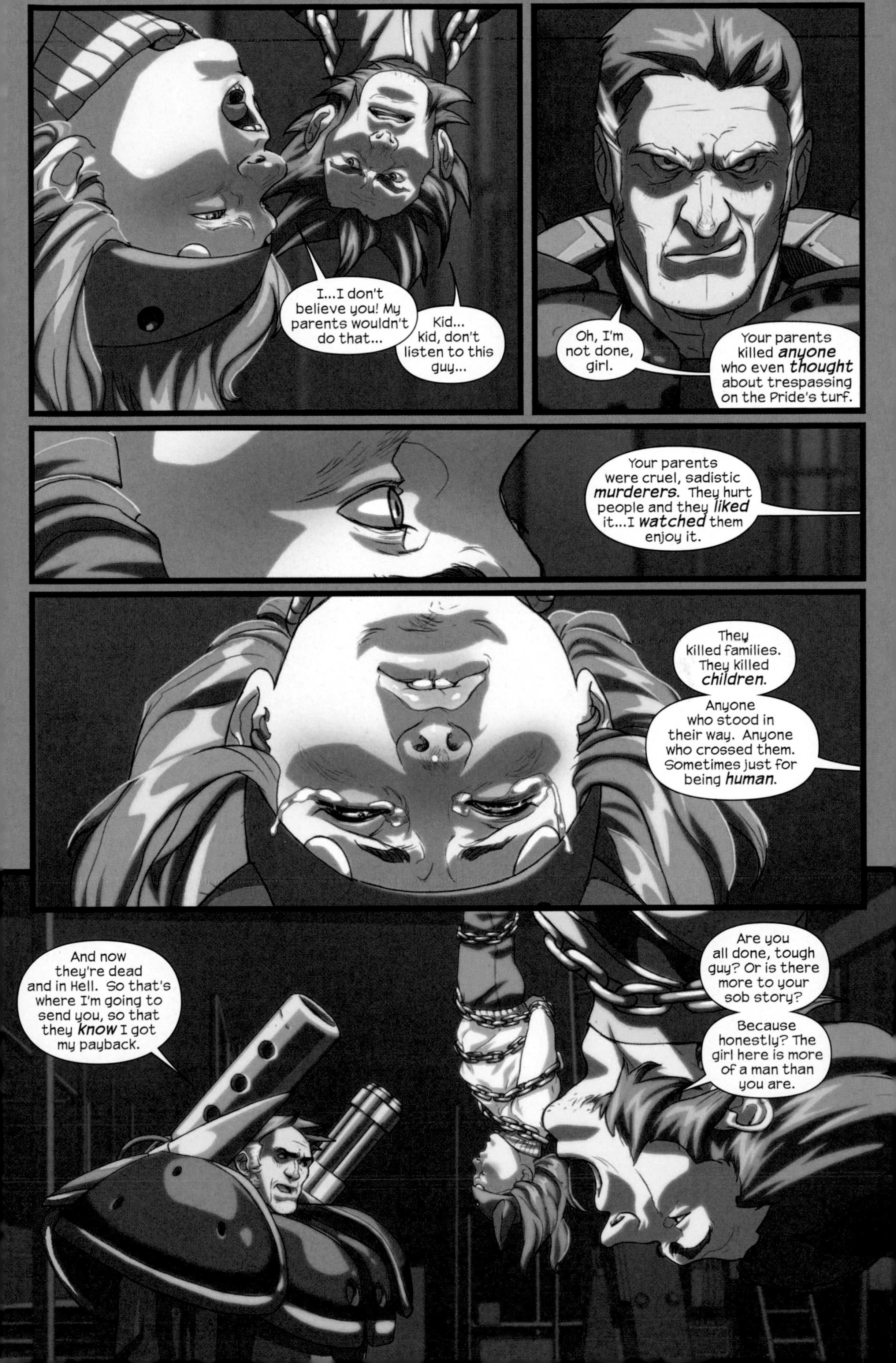
I...I don't believe you! My parents wouldn't do that...
Kid... kid, don't listen to this guy...
Oh, I'm not done, girl.
Your parents killed *anyone* who even *thought* about trespassing on the Pride's turf.
Your parents were cruel, sadistic *murderers*. They hurt people and they *liked* it...I *watched* them enjoy it.
They killed families. They killed *children*.
Anyone who stood in their way. Anyone who crossed them. Sometimes just for being *human*.
And now they're dead and in Hell. So that's where I'm going to send you, so that they *know* I got my payback.
Are you all done, tough guy? Or is there more to your sob story?
Because honestly? The girl here is more of a man than you are.

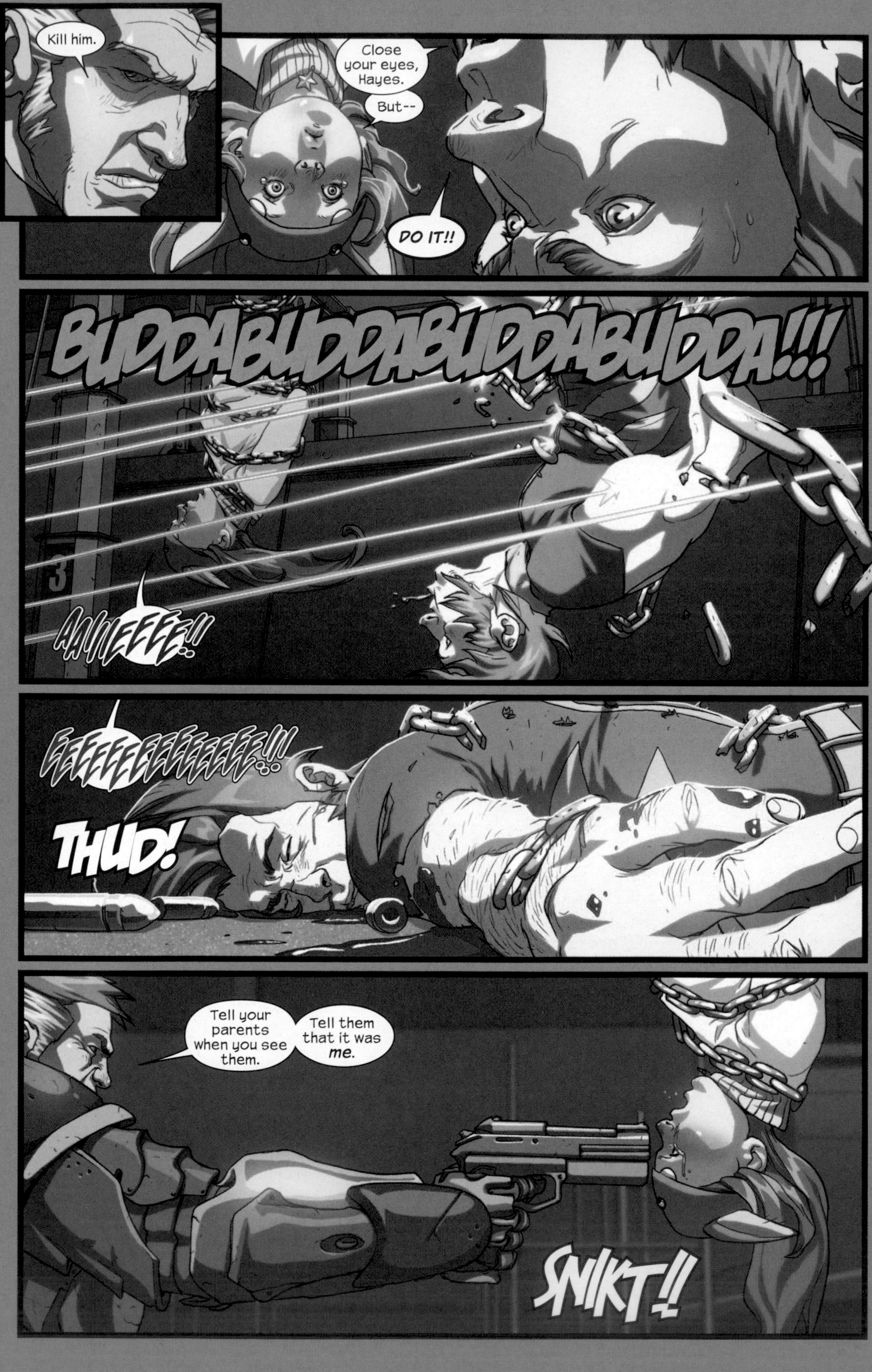
Kill him.
Close your eyes, Hayes.
But--
DO IT!!
BUDDABUDDABUDDABUDDA!!!
AAIIIEEEE!!
EEEEEEEEEEEEEE!!!
THUD!
Tell your parents when you see them.
Tell them that it was *me*.
SNIKT!!

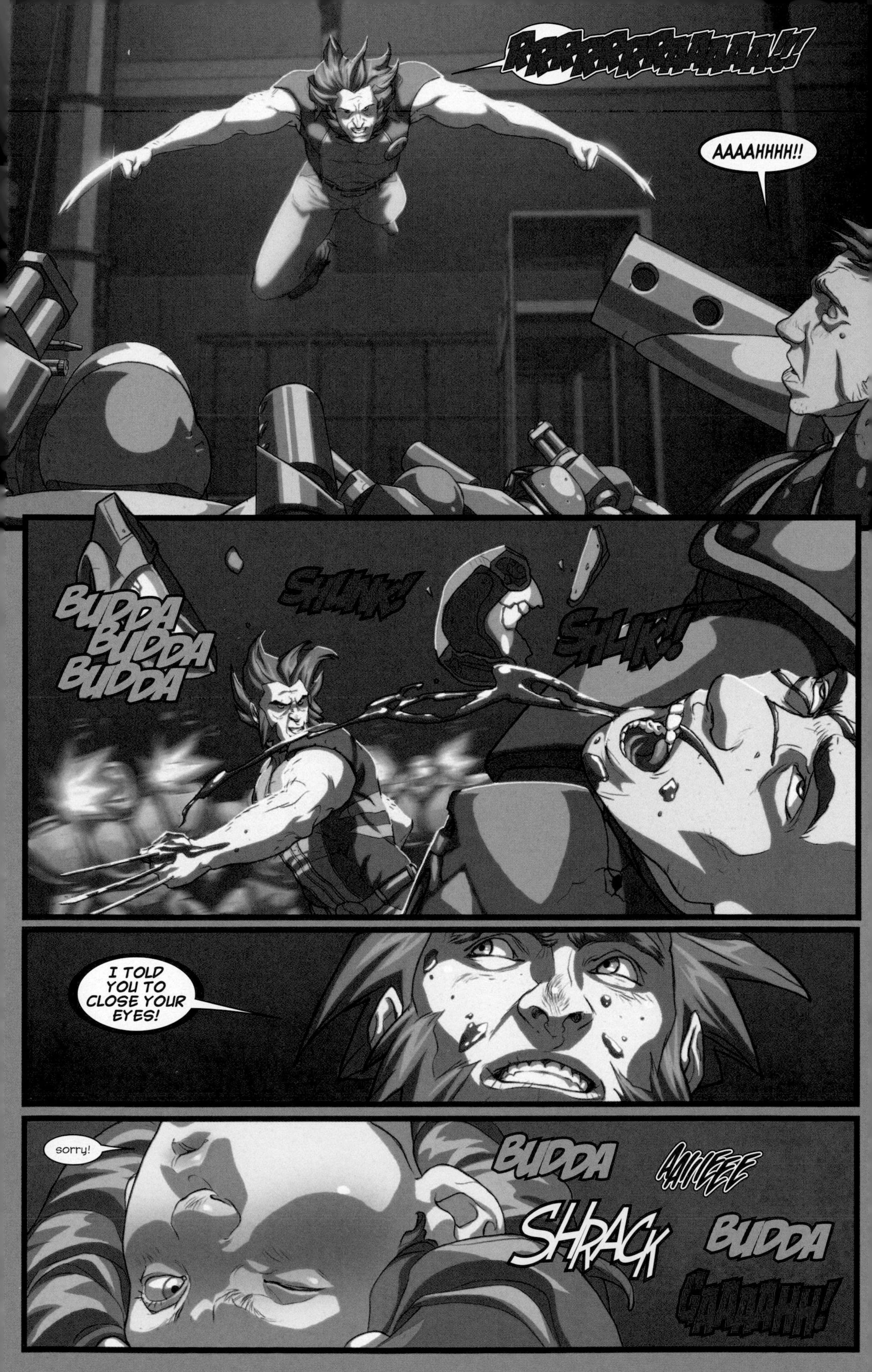
AAAAHHHH!!
BUDDA BUDDA BUDDA
SHUNK!
SHLIK!
I TOLD YOU TO CLOSE YOUR EYES!
sorry!
BUDDA
AAIIEEE
SHRACK
BUDDA

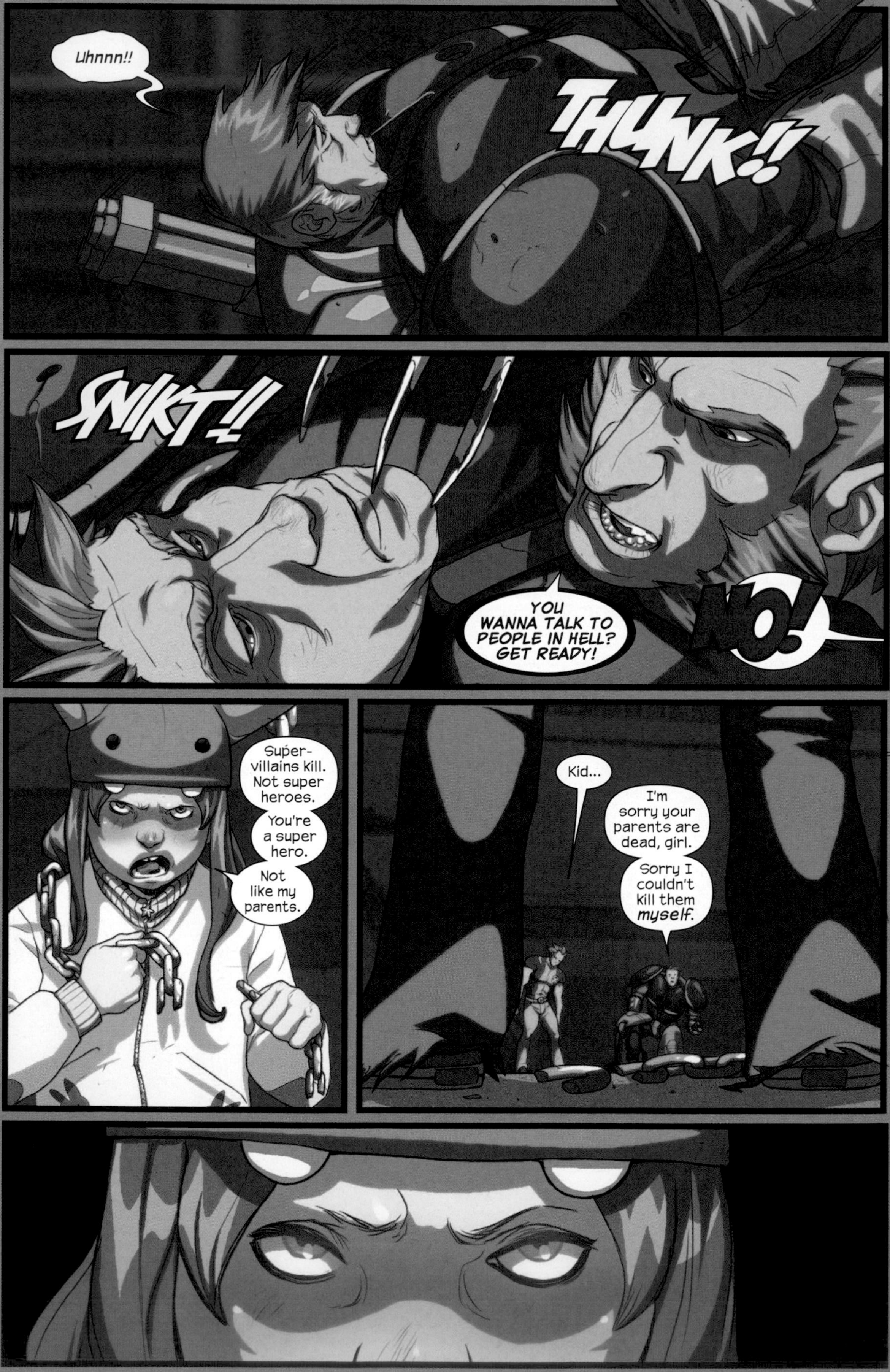
Uhnnn!!
THUNK!!
SNIKT!!
YOU WANNA TALK TO PEOPLE IN HELL? GET READY!
NO!
Super-villains kill. Not super heroes.
You're a super hero.
Not like my parents.
Kid...
I'm sorry your parents are dead, girl.
Sorry I couldn't kill them *myself*.

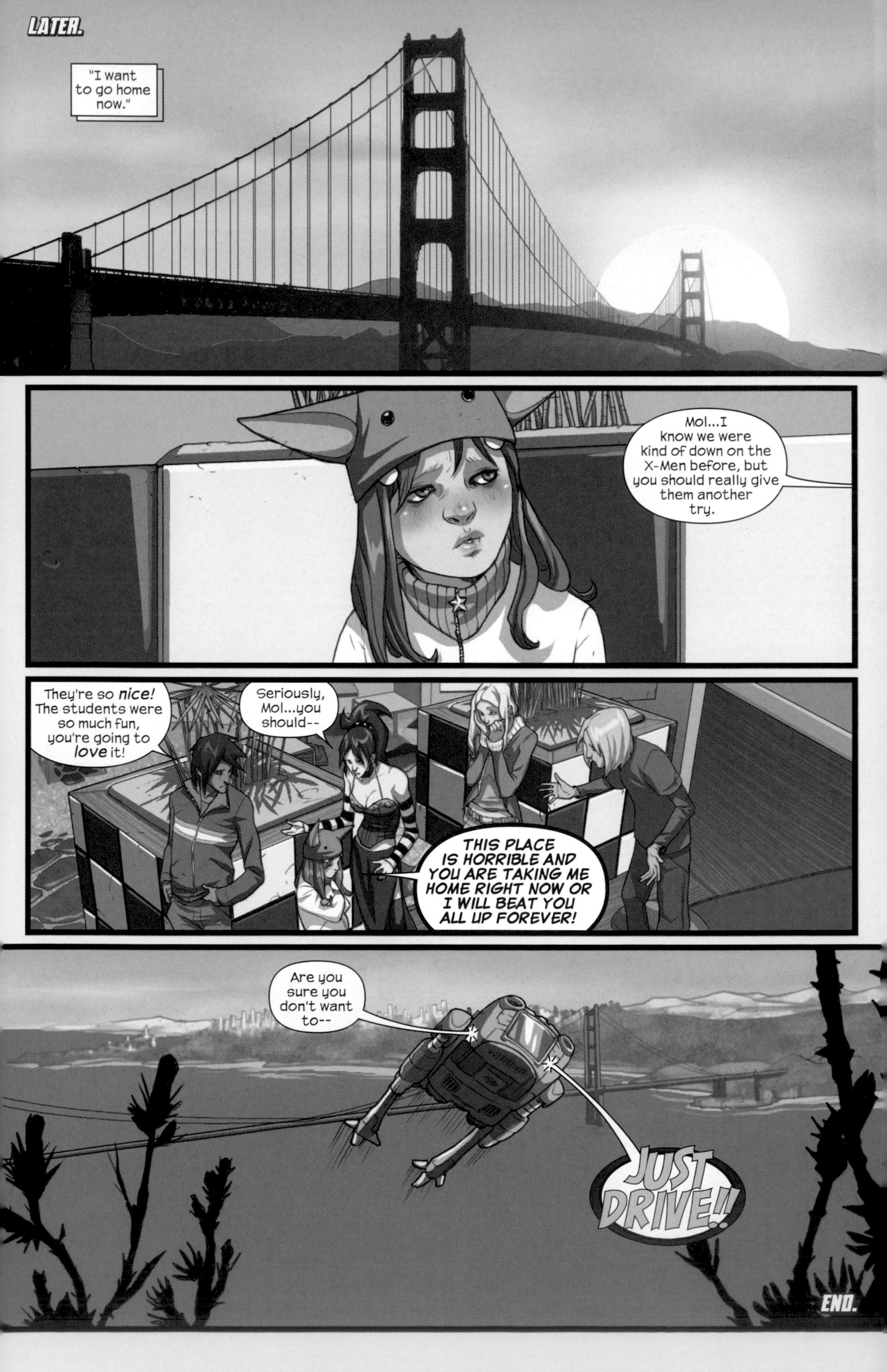
LATER.
"I want to go home now."
Mol...I know we were kind of down on the X-Men before, but you should really give them another try.
They're so *nice!* The students were so much fun, you're going to *love* it!
Seriously, Mol...you should--
THIS PLACE IS HORRIBLE AND YOU ARE TAKING ME HOME RIGHT NOW OR I WILL BEAT YOU ALL UP FOREVER!
Are you sure you don't want to--
JUST DRIVE!!
END.

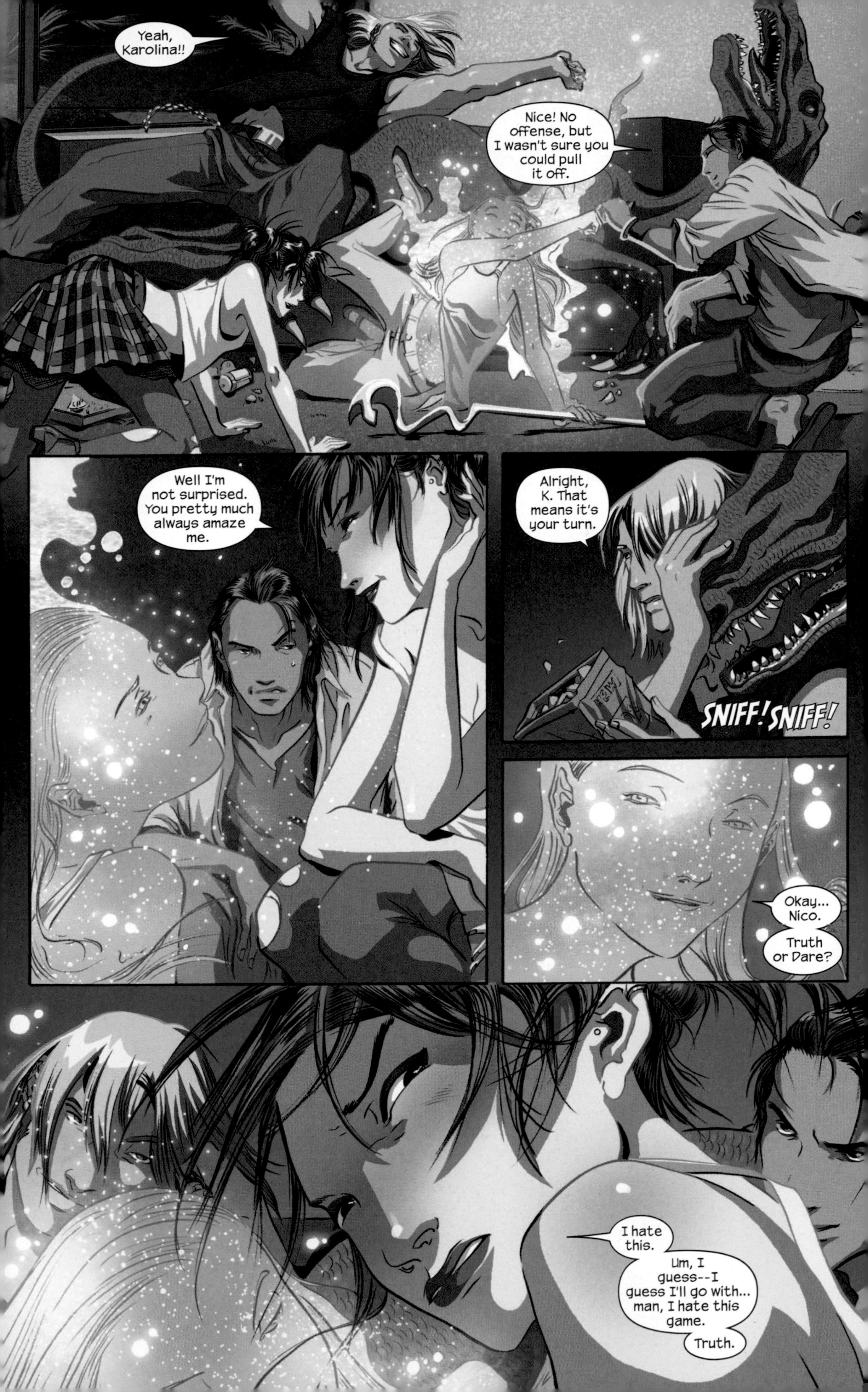
Yeah, Karolina!!
Nice! No offense, but I wasn't sure you could pull it off.
Well I'm not surprised. You pretty much always amaze me.
Alright, K. That means it's your turn.
SNIFF! SNIFF!
Okay... Nico.
Truth or Dare?
I hate this.
Um, I guess--I guess I'll go with... man, I hate this game.
Truth.

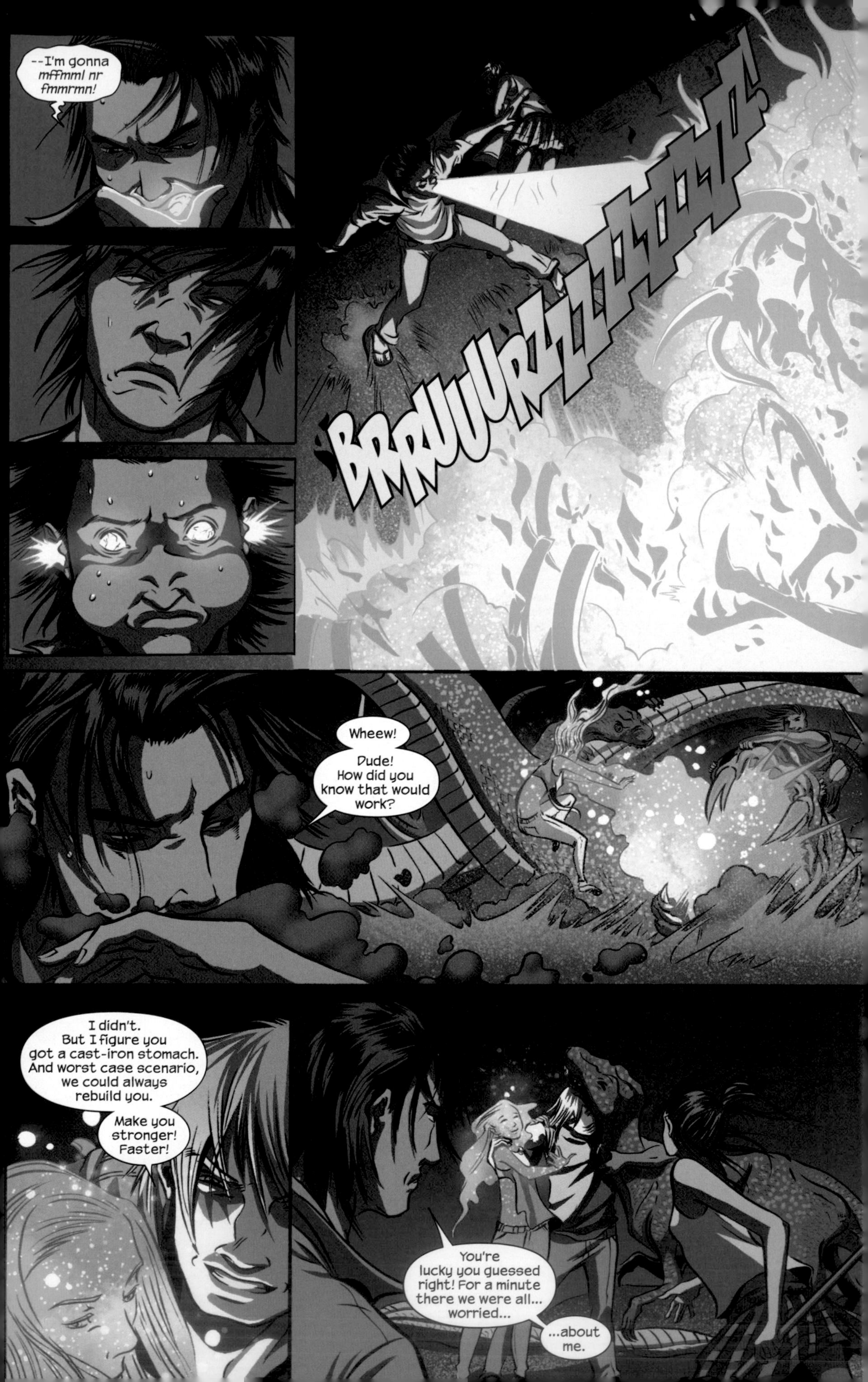

--I'm gonna *mffmml nr fmmrmn!*
BRRUUURZZZZOOZZ!
Wheew!
Dude! How did you know that would work?
I didn't. But I figure you got a cast-iron stomach. And worst case scenario, we could always rebuild you.
Make you stronger! Faster!
You're lucky you guessed right! For a minute there we were all... worried...
...about me.

THE END.

9
VARIANT BY
DAVID LAFUENTE

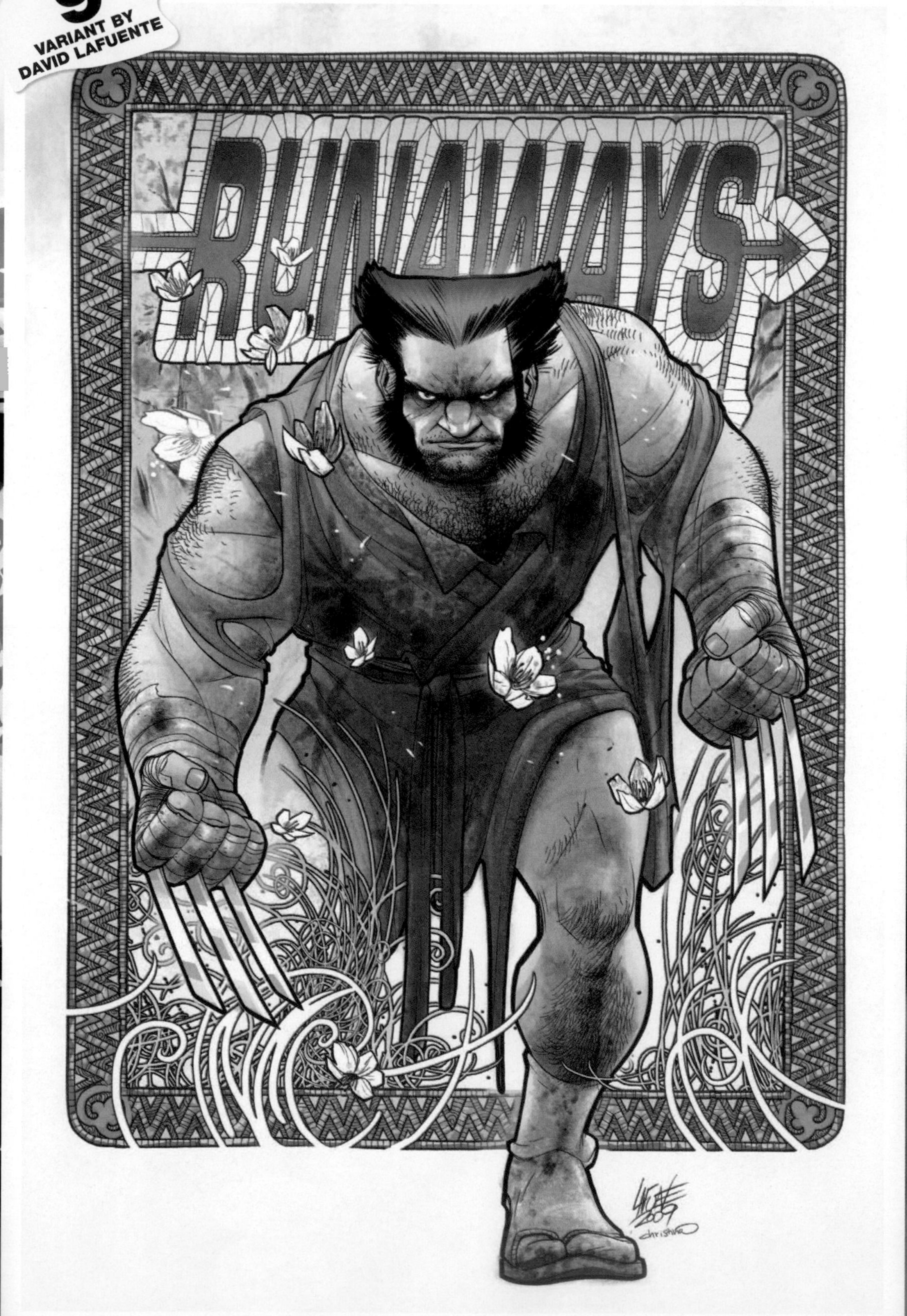
RUNAWAYS

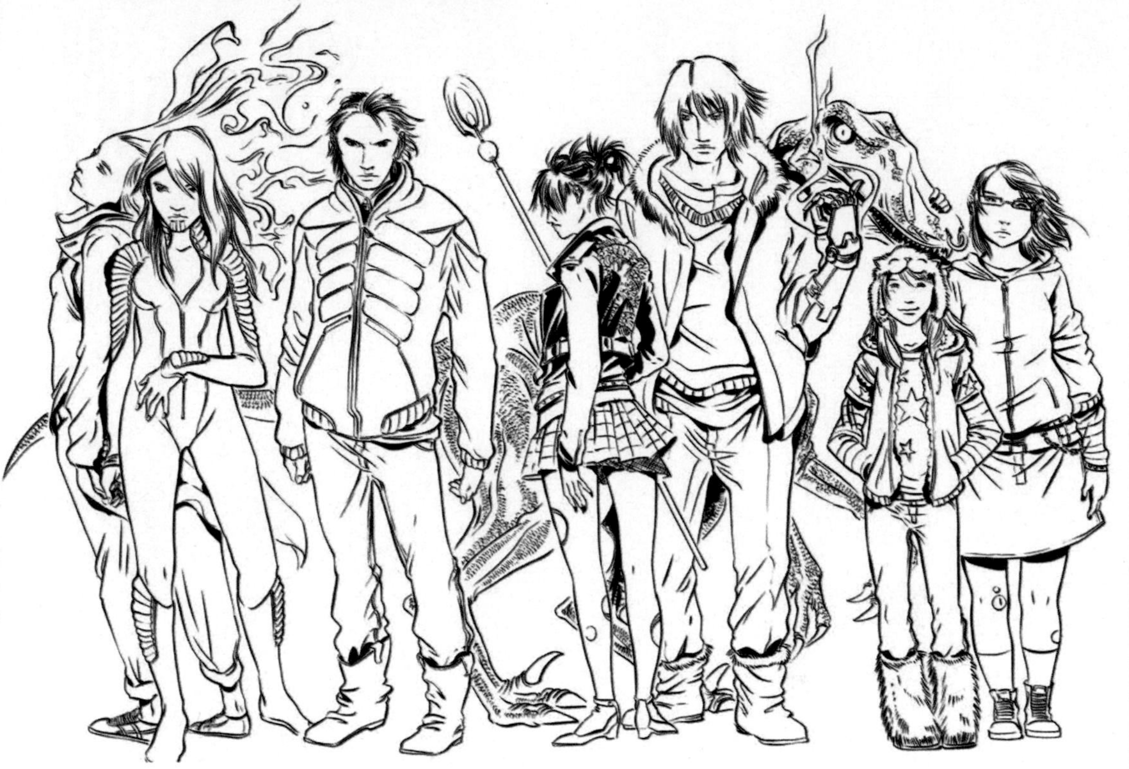

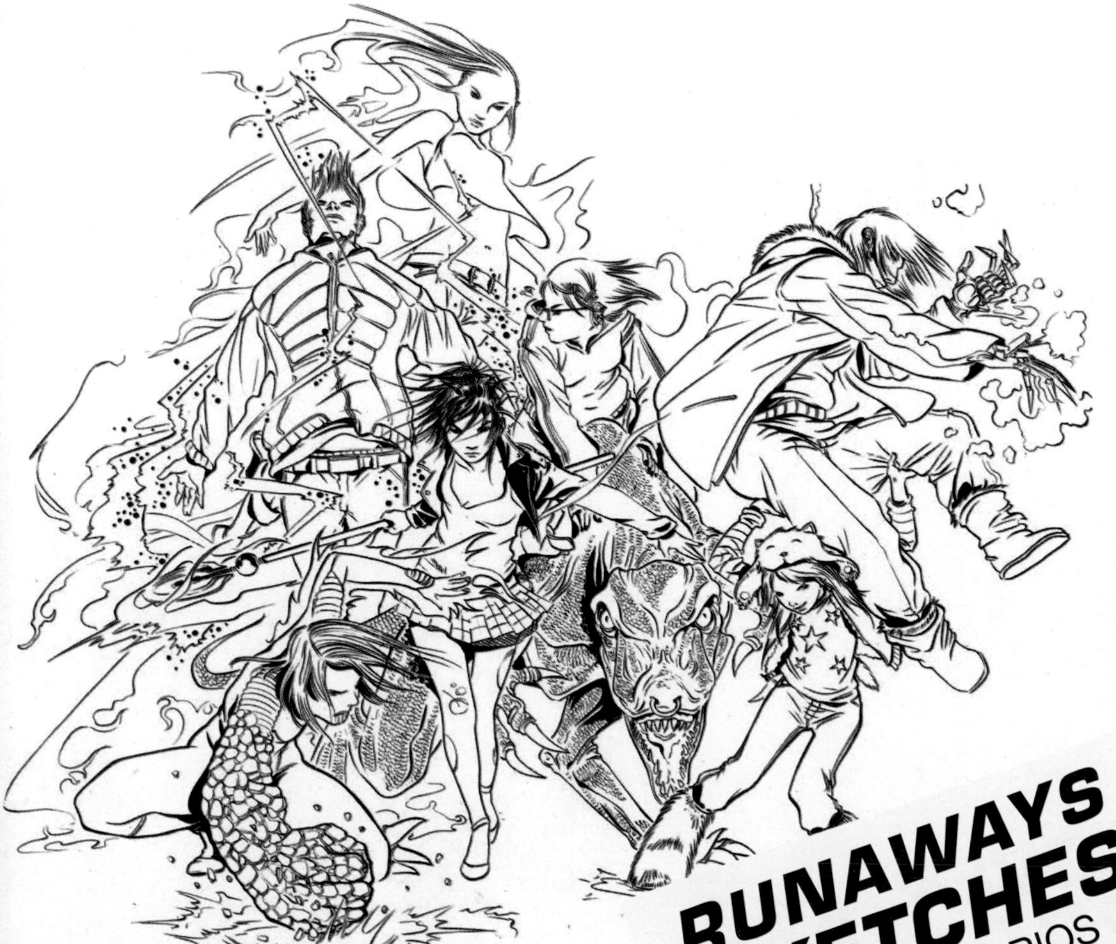

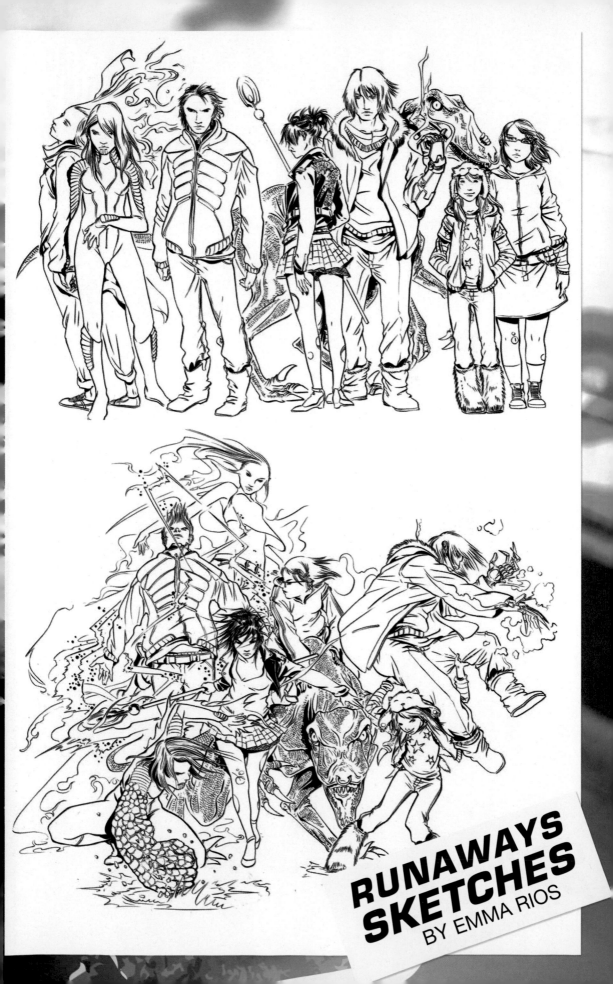

RUNAWAYS SKETCHES
BY EMMA RIOS

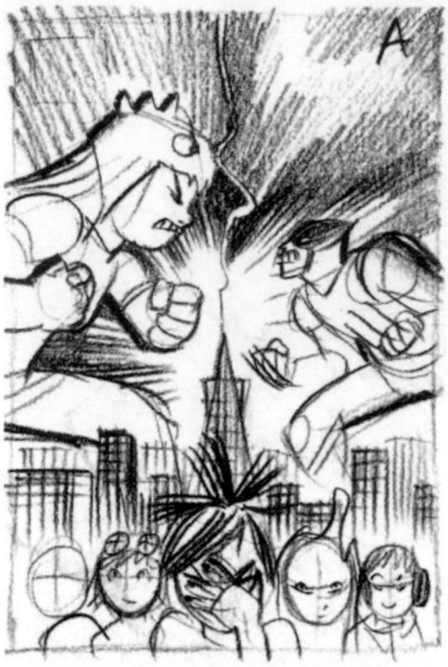
A

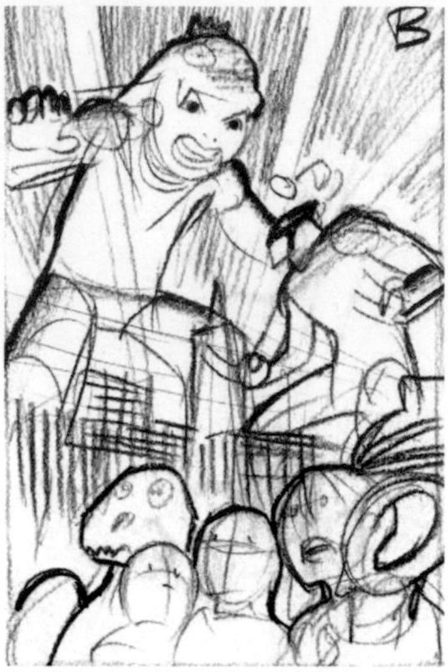
B

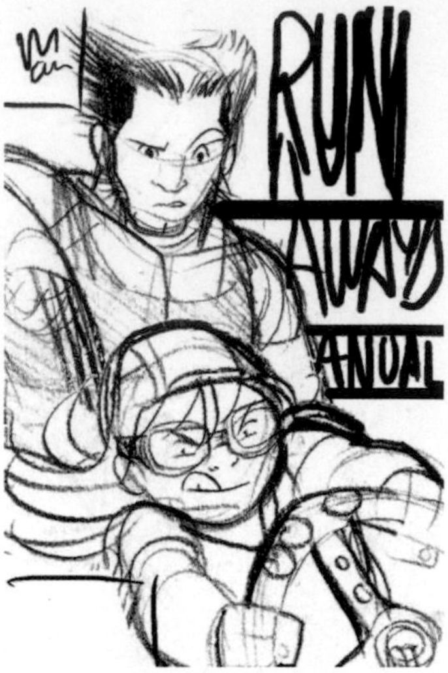
RUN
AWAYS
ANUAL

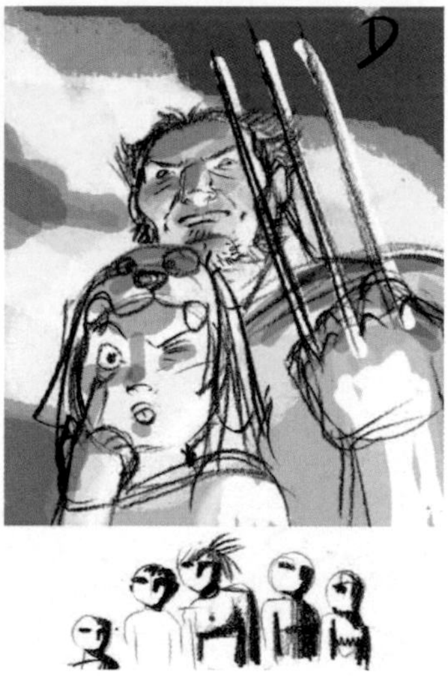
D

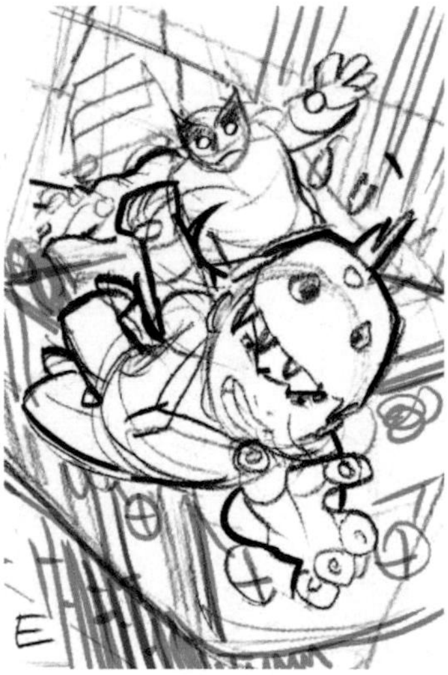
E

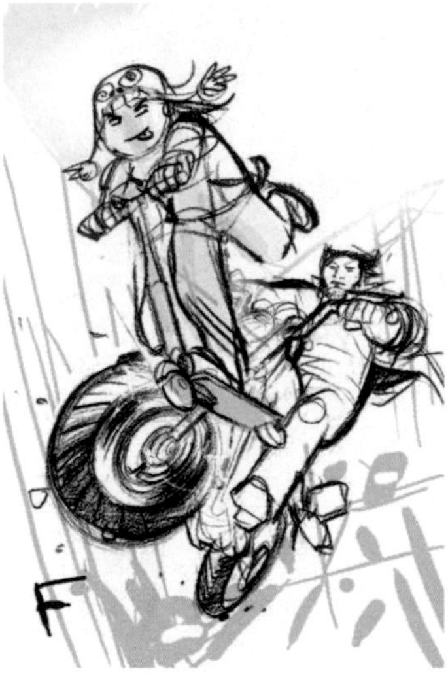
F

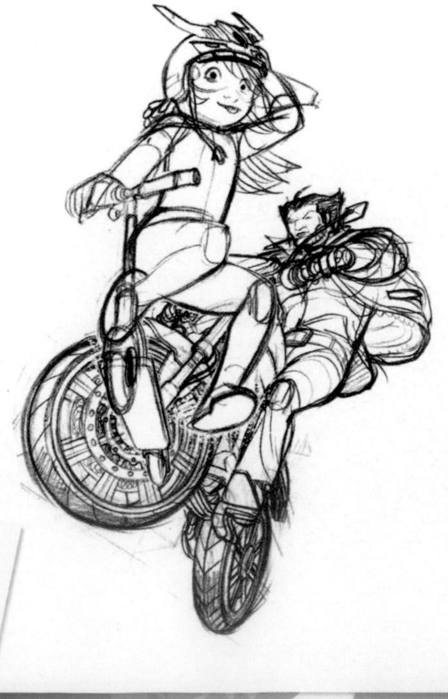

COVER #10 PROCESS
BY DAVID LAFUENTE

INKS

ALTERNATE COLORS

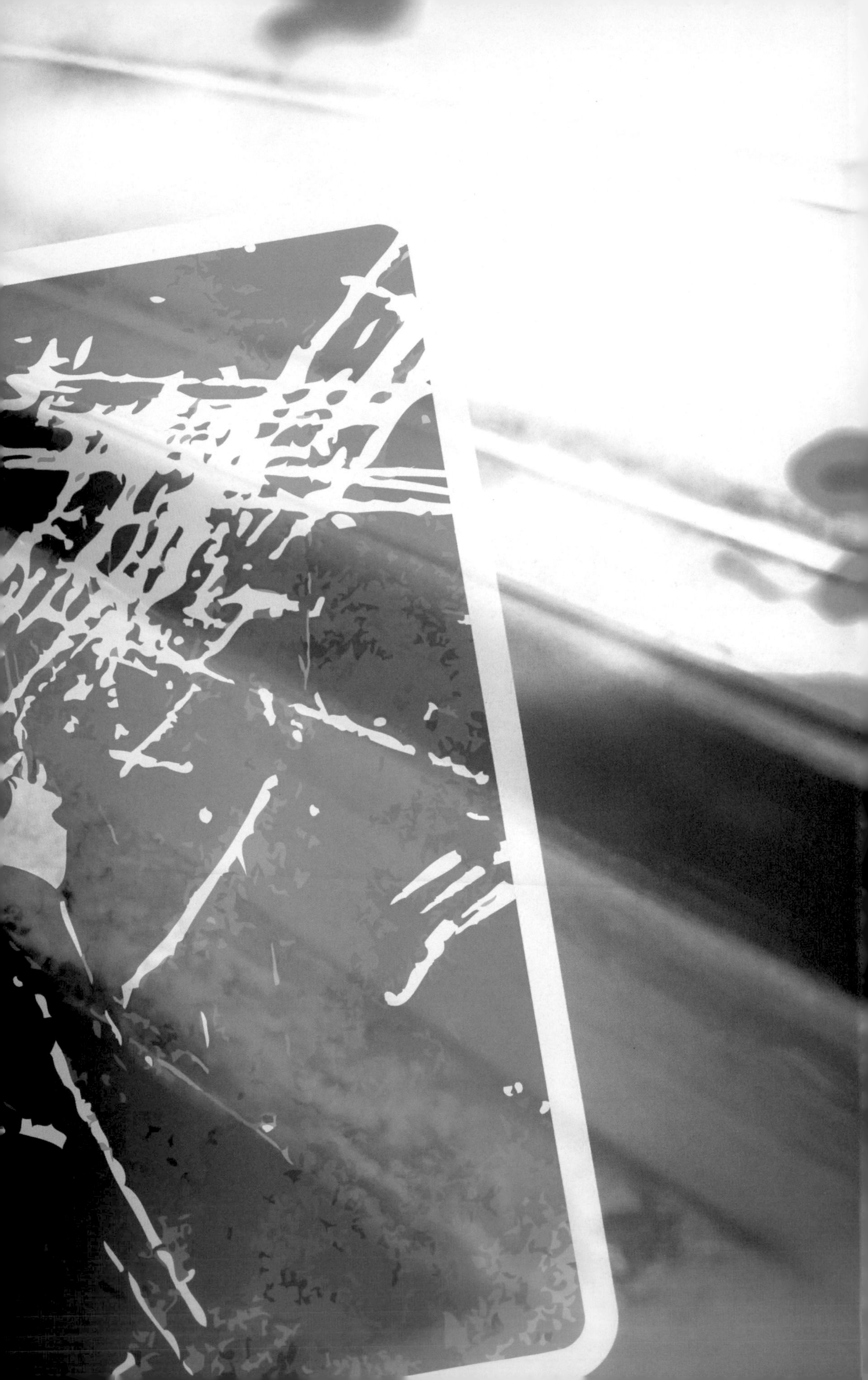